the winter garden

a seasonal guide to making the most of your garden

the winter garden

Richard Rosenfeld

LORENZ BOOKS

This edition is published by Lorenz Books

Lorenz Books is an imprint of Anness Publishing Limited
Hermes House, 88–89 Blackfriars Road, London SE1 8HA
tel. 020 7401 2077; fax 020 7633 9499
www.lorenzbooks.com; info@anness.com

Published in the USA by Lorenz Books, Anness Publishing Inc.,
27 West 20th Street, New York, NY 10011; fax 212 807 6813

Published in Australia by Lorenz Books, Anness Publishing Pty Ltd.,
tel. (02) 8920 8622; fax (02) 8920 8633

This edition distributed in the UK by Aurum Press Ltd.,
tel. 020 7637 3225; fax 020 7580 2469

This edition distributed in the USA by National Book Network,
tel. 301 459 3366; fax 301 459 1705; www.nbnbooks.com

This edition distributed in Canada by General Publishing,
tel. 416 445 3333; fax 416 445 5991; www.genpub.com

This edition distributed in New Zealand by David Bateman Ltd
tel. (09) 415 7664; fax (09) 415 8892

A CIP catalogue record for this book is available from the British Library.

10 9 8 7 6 5 4 3 2 1

Publisher: Joanna Lorenz
Managing Editor: Judith Simons
Senior Editor: Doreen Palamartschuk
Art Manager: Clare Reynolds
Additional text: Kathy Brown, Andrew Mikolajski and Peter McHoy
Designer: WhiteLight
Photographers: Peter Anderson, Caroline Arber, Jonathan Buckley, Michelle Garratt,
    David Markson and Peter McHoy.
Production Controller: Joanna King

page 1 The flowers of *Crocus tommasinianus*, emerging through dew-drenched grass.
page 2 Winter-flowering heathers provide a welcome burst of colour.
page 3 Fragrant viburnum flowers are borne even when snow is on the ground.
pages 4–5 *Galanthus nivalis* (snowdrops) are the archetypal winter flower.

Note
In the directory section of this book, each plant is given a hardiness rating.
The temperature ranges are as follows:
frost tender – may be damaged by temperatures below 5°C (41°F);
half-hardy – can withstand temperatures down to 0°C (32°F);
frost hardy – can withstand temperatures down to -5°C (23°F);
fully hardy – can withstand temperatures down to -15°C (5°F).

CONTENTS

INTRODUCTION

Winter gardens can be extraordinarily beautiful. They may lack beds and borders overflowing with colourful summer flowers and verdant foliage, but they often have a subtler, more satisfying attraction. There is, of course, no lack of colour if you look closely. Many trees and shrubs bear vivid red, yellow or orange berries, and there are plenty of bulbs that flower in the depths of winter. Evergreen plants and conifers provide form and texture in every shade of green. It is in winter, however, that the underlying structure of the garden can be appreciated. The materials and shapes of unclothed pergolas and trellises can be admired, while ornaments, such as terracotta urns and stone sundials, can be enjoyed for themselves.

left Hellebores, which are available in a wide range of colours, produce a superb winter display. Grow them in large clumps for a striking effect.

right *Cornus alba* 'Sibirica' is one of the best dogwoods for bright winter colour. Give it a sunny, prominent position.

WINTER GARDENS CAN EASILY BE BRIGHTENED up. When you are planning your garden, think about the effect that you want to achieve in winter, not just about how the individual plant will look when it is in full bloom or leaf. Most herbaceous perennials die back in autumn, but there is a vast range of other plants, from trees and shrubs, both deciduous and evergreen, to tiny bulbs, that can be used to provide interest all winter long.

choosing colour

The winter garden can be a mass of colour. Early-flowering bulbs, such as *Crocus sieberi* and its cultivars, can be allowed to naturalize in grass to provide a carpet of colour. In late winter, the tiny *Iris reticulata* has rich purple flowers, splashed with yellow.

below The easily grown, 12cm (5in) high *Iris* 'George' starts flowering at the end of winter.

I. danfordiae, another early flowerer, has scented yellow blooms. *I. foetidissima* has bright red winter seeds, and with luck the violet-blue *I. unguicularis* (syn. *I. stylosa*) might be in flower before Christmas day if there has been a long, hot summer.

Colourful berries abound on many forms of cotoneaster and holly. If they are not eaten by birds, the red berries of *Cotoneaster horizontalis* last until midwinter, and the yellow berries of *C. salicifolius* 'Rothschildianus' last well into winter. If you want holly berries, make sure you plant both male and female forms or a self-fertile form.

fragrant flowers

High summer may be the time of roses, lavender and honeysuckle, but among the delights of a well-planned winter garden will be the subtle aromas of carefully selected shrubs and bulbs, all the more welcome for being unexpected. Look out especially for viburnums and daphnes. The deciduous *Viburnum* x *bodnantense*, for example, bears strongly scented white to pink flowers from autumn to spring, while the evergreen *Daphne odora* has clusters of fragrant, purplish-pink to white flowers from midwinter to spring.

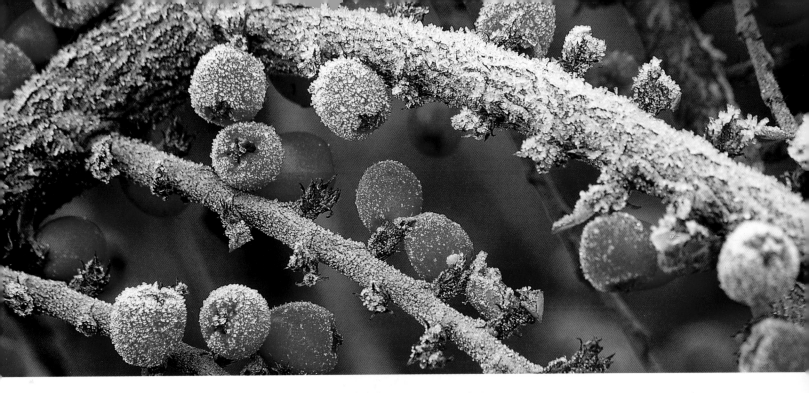

The reliable *Hamamelis* spp. (witch hazel) produce their unusual, spidery but scented flowers on the leafless branches from early winter into late spring, seemingly unaffected by the harshest of weather. Less well known is *Sarcococca humilis* (sweet box). Plant this evergreen shrub near a path or door so that you can enjoy the sweet scent of the pink-flushed, white flowers in midwinter.

beautiful bark

It is easy to overlook the attractive bark of many trees, which is often visible only in winter. Perhaps the most exciting of the trees with interesting bark is the compact *Prunus serrula*. It has smooth, rich red-brown bark, which peels to reveal gold-coloured bands.

Tilia platyphyllus 'Rubra' (red-twigged lime) also provides vibrant winter colour. The mass of bright red, twiggy growth at the top of the tree looks sensational when the ground below is covered with snow. Among the best of the white-barked trees is the lovely birch, *Betula utilis* var. *jacquemontii* 'Silver Shadow'. Look out, too, for shrubs with colourful shoots. One of the best is *Cornus alba* (red-barked dogwood), which has extraordinary, bright red new stems.

above Bright frost-covered red berries of *Cotoneaster frigidus* 'Cornubia'.

left There is room for the shiny, brown-stemmed *Prunus serrula* even in a medium-sized garden. Grow it as a feature plant where it can be easily seen.

WINTER
PLANTS

The best way to see the full range of winter plants is to visit a well-stocked garden centre or nursery between the end of autumn and early spring. It is also worth visiting well-maintained, first-rate public gardens. Take a notebook with you so that you do not forget the plants that appeal to you. Some of the best known and most reliable bulbs, perennials and shrubs are described and illustrated on the following pages. There is also advice on where and how to grow them so that you get the best results every time.

left *Cornus stolonifera* 'Flaviramea' is a great choice for winter gardens because of its bright yellow, vertical stems. Grow plenty of clumps together for the most startling effect.

above *Crocus chrysanthus* 'Blue Pearl'.

bulbs

There are many excellent bulbs for the winter garden. Always plant them in groups or, in a large garden, in drifts so they can naturalize.

Chionodoxa

Commonly known as glory of the snow, this is a genus of six species of bulbs found on mountainsides and forests in Crete, western Turkey and Cyprus. They are related to scillas. *Chionodoxa forbesii* 'Pink Giant' produces racemes of 4 to 12 star-shaped, pale pink flowers, 1–2cm (½–¾in) wide, with white centres.
Flowering height 15cm (6in)
Flowering time Late winter to mid-spring
Hardiness Fully hardy

Crocus

The crocus is one of the best-known late winter and early spring flowers. The genus embraces more than 80 species of dwarf corms found in a wide variety of locations, from central and southern Europe, northern Africa and the Middle East to central Asia and western China. Hundreds of cultivars have been produced. Almost every flower colour but pink is available, and some are attractively striped. A few have stamens in a contrasting colour. Robust hybrids are splendid for naturalizing in lawns, and they can create stunning effects, either in the traditional mixture of colours or when a more subtle selection of just one or two shades is planted.

C. chrysanthus

This species is usually represented in cultivation by its many selections, all flowering in late winter to early spring and including 'Advance', yellow with violet outer petals; 'Blue Pearl', which has silver-blue flowers; 'Ladykiller', which has slender, pure white flowers marked with purple; 'Snow Bunting', pure white; and one of the most spectacular cultivars, 'Zwanenburg Bronze', which has rich yellow flowers marked with purple-brown.
Flowering height To 7.5cm (3in)
Flowering time Late winter to early spring
Hardiness Fully hardy

C. sieberi

Flowering in late winter to early spring, this species has yellow-centred, light blue flowers with bright orange pistils. Among the prettiest forms are the golden-throated, white 'Albus' (syn. 'Bowles' White'),

below left to right
Chionodoxa forbesii 'Pink Giant', *Crocus tommasinianus* 'Ruby Giant' and *Crocus sieberi* 'Firefly'.

which flowers in early spring, and 'Firefly', which has prolific lilac and yellow flowers.
Flowering height To 7.5cm (3in)
Flowering time Late winter to early spring
Hardiness Fully hardy

C. tommasinianus

This crocus is one of the best for naturalizing and produces lavender flowers in late winter. 'Ruby Giant' has large, purple flowers; 'Whitewell Purple' has purplish-red flowers, but with silvery-mauve lining inside and it is more slender than those of 'Ruby Giant'.
Flowering height To 10cm (4in)
Flowering time Late winter to early spring
Hardiness Fully hardy

C. vernus

The species has many selections, all of which are excellent for naturalizing and flower from late winter to early spring. These include 'Jeanne d'Arc', which has pure white flowers; 'Pickwick', which has greyish-white flowers, striped with violet; and 'Remembrance', which has violet flowers with a silvery sheen.
Flowering height To 10cm (4in)
Flowering time Late winter to early spring
Hardiness Fully hardy

Cyclamen

The unmistakable flowers of these plants make a delightful carpet under deciduous trees and shrubs.

C. coum

This species flowers from late winter to mid-spring, in a range of colours, from purple-violet to pink and white. The nodding flowers often have darker staining towards the mouth. The attractive rounded leaves usually have silver markings. This species associates particularly well with snowdrops.
Flowering height 5–7.5cm (2–3in)
Flowering time Late winter
Hardiness Fully hardy

C. persicum

The scented flowers range in colour from white to a glowing cerise-red and appear in winter and spring. Some combine two colours on the frilly petals. The flowers have darker staining towards the mouth, and the heart-shaped leaves are often patterned. Many cultivars have been bred but look for those with a sweet scent and attractively marked foliage.
Flowering height 10–20cm (4–8in)
Flowering time Early winter to early spring
Hardiness Frost tender

above left to right This group of mixed crocuses, which includes *Crocus tommasinianus, C. chrysanthus* and *C. vernus,* has formed a natural-looking carpet of colour; *Cyclamen persicum* and *C. coum.*

below *Crocus sieberi* 'Albus' (syn. 'Bowles' White').

Eranthis

Commonly known as winter aconite, this is one of the earliest bulbs to flower. They are robust enough to penetrate a light covering of snow, which is a charming effect when it occurs. Like snowdrops, they transplant best when putting on growth after flowering, so when buying them look for plants "in the green". They are good for carpeting areas beneath deciduous trees. The flowers open only when the sun is shining. They soon form large clumps and naturalize quickly in ideal conditions, especially in alkaline soils.

The golden petals of *Eranthis hyemalis* are surrounded by a collar of deeply dissected green leaves.
Flowering height 5–7.5cm (2–3in)
Flowering time Winter
Hardiness Fully hardy

Galanthus

Few plants have the charm of the snowdrop or are as welcome. Each flower has six petals, the outer three longer than the inner ones. Unusually among bulbs, snowdrops seem to prefer slightly damp soil. Snowdrops associate well with winter aconite, winter-flowering heathers and dwarf *Reticulata* irises.

G. elwesii

This species is less well known than *G. nivalis*. It is a larger plant, with bright green, strap-shaped leaves and flowers with large green spots on the inner petals.
Flowering height 25cm (10in)
Flowering time Winter
Hardiness Fully hardy

G. nivalis

The best-known of the snowdrops and one that naturalizes easily. The bell-shaped, pure white flowers hang downwards, the outer petals flaring outwards to

reveal the green markings on the inner ones. 'Flore Pleno', the double form, is no less charming.

Flowering height 10cm (4in)
Flowering time Winter
Hardiness Fully hardy

G. 'S. Arnott'

Long, virgin-white flowers fall like rounded drops of snow from a slender stem. The three outer petals open to reveal three shorter inner petals, each with green markings at the base and apex.

Flowering height 2–4cm (¾–1½in)
Flowering time Late winter
Hardiness Fully hardy

Iris

This genus has more than 300 species of winter-, spring- and summer-flowering bulbs, rhizomes and perennials.

I. danfordiae

A dwarf species with scented, yellow flowers, 5cm (2in) across, which have green markings. They look effective with winter-flowering heathers.

Flowering height 10cm (4in)
Flowering time Late winter to early spring
Hardiness Fully hardy

I. reticulata

This dainty species from the Caucasus is one of the first bulbous plants to flower in the gardening year, producing its rich violet-blue, yellow-splashed flowers in late winter. Unfortunately, it is not reliably perennial, so plant fresh stock annually. Selections include 'George', which has deep purple flowers with a yellow stripe down the centre of the fall petal.

Flowering height 15cm (6in)
Flowering time Late winter
Hardiness Fully hardy

I. unguicularis

Algerian iris (syn. *I. stylosa*) is one of the harbingers of spring. It is unique in the genus and should be planted in every winter garden. Among the grassy foliage, elegant lilac-mauve flowers with yellow markings unfurl from scrolled buds as early as midwinter, the main flowering being in late winter to early spring. It needs a hot spot in well-drained soil: at the foot of a warm wall is ideal. For reliable flowering, the upper surface of the rhizome should be exposed to the sun and plants should be left undisturbed once established.

Flowering height 23–30cm (9–12in)
Flowering time Late winter to early spring
Hardiness Fully hardy

above *Iris danfordiae.*

below left to right
Iris reticulata 'George', *I. r.* 'Pauline' has dark violet flowers with distinctive white markings on the falls, and *I. unguicularis.*

above Hellebores flower in a wide range of colours.

below left to right *Helleborus* covered in snow and *H. orientalis.*

perennials

Most perennials are dormant in winter and start shooting out of the ground in spring, so the ones that do flower in winter are eye-catching. The following provide an exciting glimpse of what can be grown in the winter garden, when many plants are resting.

Helleborus

This is an important genus from the gardener's point of view, with many desirable plants, all with nodding flowers and handsome, more or less evergreen leaves. They are indispensable in the winter garden. All hellebores thrive in the shade of deciduous trees and shrubs and will even tolerate heavy shade next to a wall. They are easy to grow in any fertile, well-drained soil (although most prefer heavy and alkaline conditions) in sun or shade. All are poisonous.

H. argutifolius

Corsican hellebore is a handsome species that tolerates drier conditions than most other members of the genus. The firm, jade-green leaves, which have toothed leaflets, are attractive throughout the year.

The clusters of apple-green, cup-shaped flowers appear in late winter and last until early spring. It is a splendid foil for *Iris reticulata* and early narcissi.
Flowering height 1m (3ft)
Flowering time Late winter and early spring
Hardiness Fully hardy

H. foetidus

Bear's foot or stinking hellebore is a dramatic species, which makes a clump of dark-green leaves. Strong stems carrying many bell-shaped, apple-green flowers (usually edged with maroon) appear in midwinter to mid-spring. It looks good with snowdrops. Plants of the Wester Flisk Group have red-tinged stems and leaf and flower stalks and grey-tinged leaves.
Flowering height 75cm (30in)
Flowering time Midwinter to mid-spring
Hardiness Fully hardy

H. niger

The Christmas rose is one of the prettiest and most desirable of the hellebores, but unfortunately, it is also one of the trickiest to grow. It has dark green, basal, leathery leaves and large, glistening, cup-shaped white flowers in early winter. The flowers are sometimes

flushed with pink, with greenish-white centres, ageing to pinkish-white. It is slow to establish and needs fertile, sticky soil that does not dry out. 'Potter's Wheel' is a desirable selection with larger flowers, as is *H. niger* subsp. *macranthus* with its bluish or grey-green leaves.

Flowering height 30cm (12in)
Flowering time Early winter to early spring
Hardiness Fully hardy

H. orientalis

The Lenten rose, an Eastern Mediterranean species, is one of the easiest hellebores to grow and is also one of the most variable species. The flowers, which appear from late winter into spring, can be white, yellowish-cream, dusky-pink, clear glowing red or plum-purple, and they can also be spotted inside with a different colour to varying degrees. All are flushed green inside and out. The leaves are also handsome: firm and with serrated edges, and in shades of green, paler leaves being associated with paler flower colours. Blackened leaves should be removed. Plant in clusters of 3–5 plants to make a striking statement.

Flowering height 45cm (18in)
Flowering time Midwinter to mid-spring
Hardiness Fully hardy

Ophiopogon

The species, *Ophiopogon planiscapus* (lilyturf), is rarely grown: it is a grass-like plant with dull, deep-green leaves and small, bell-shaped, pale pinkish-purple summer flowers, and produces small, black berries in autumn. Of greater interest are the cultivars, especially 'Nigrescens' (syn. *O.* 'Arabiscus'; 'Black Dragon'; 'Ebony Knight'), with striking, black-purple leaves and small, purplish, bell-shaped flowers. The plant spreads slowly by stolons. For the most impact, grow it in gravel or in containers. It is especially effective in a Japanese-style planting.

Flowering height 20cm (8in)
Flowering time Summer (winter leaves)
Hardiness Fully hardy

Phormium

Originally from New Zealand, phormiums look exotic but are frost hardy. Being evergreen, they add interest throughout the year. *P. tenax* 'Rainbow Queen' has a wide range of colours with its sword-like leaves ranging from pink and lemon through orange and bronze. It requires sun and moist soil.

Height 2–2.5m (7–8ft)
Flowering time Summer (winter leaves)
Hardiness Frost hardy

above left to right
Ophiopogon planiscapus 'Nigrescens', *Helleborus niger* 'Potter's Wheel' and *Phormium tenax* 'Rainbow Queen'.

grasses

above *Carex buchananii.*

Grasses have four good seasons of interest: in spring, when the bright new shoots start emerging, in summer, when they are at their peak and flower, in autumn, when many turn yellow and reddish, and in winter, because they should be left standing, so that their shapes add interest until being cut down at the end of the season.

Carex

Sedge is a large and important genus, containing about 1000 species, which are distinguished by their triangular stems. They are ideal bog garden plants, but some are also worth trying in mixed borders for their attractive mounds of leaves. Most are best in reliably moist soil in sun or light shade. *C. buchananii* is an elegant, clump-forming evergreen with narrow copper-coloured leaves that turn towards orange in the winter. *C. comans* 'Frosted Curls' is an evergreen, compact hybrid, which makes dense clumps of narrow, pale green leaves that curl at the tips. *C. conica* is from Japan and South Korea and is usually seen in gardens in an attractive form, C. c. 'Snowline', which makes neat clumps of dark green leaves strikingly margined

below left to right *Carex hachijoensis 'Evergold', Elymus magellanicus* and *Carex flagellifera.*

with white. This does well in ordinary garden soil and is useful for providing long-term interest at the front of a border; it is also effective in gravel. *C. flagellifera* makes a clump of arching, bronze-brown leaves, which are an excellent foil to green-, silver- or yellow-leaved plants. It will grow in almost any soil. *C. oshimensis* 'Evergold' (syn. *C. morrowii* 'Evergold') is an outstanding evergreen sedge with arching leaves, centrally banded with cream. It is an excellent plant for lighting up a winter garden. It prefers well-drained soil but will grow in sun or semi-shade. *C. testacea* is an evergreen sedge from New Zealand. The arching, pale olive-green leaves are tinged bronze.
Flowering height 30–60cm (12–24in)
Flowering time Midsummer (winter leaves)
Hardiness Borderline to fully hardy

Elymus

Wild rye or lyme grass is excellent as an infill in mixed or herbaceous borders. Grow these grasses in ordinary garden soil in sun or light shade. *E. magellanicus* is a clump-forming species, native to Chile and Argentina, and has spiky, steel-blue leaves. It is a good container plant.
Flowering height 15cm (6in)
Flowering time Summer (winter leaves)
Hardiness Fully hardy

Festuca

The genus contains about 300 perennial grasses, which produce attractive tufts of foliage. They are ideal for placing at the front of borders or among rock plants. *F. glauca*, blue or grey fescue, is one of the most popular grasses. It is an evergreen species, which makes tufts of steely-blue leaves that are still evident in winter. The summer flowers are an added bonus. It can also be grown in containers. It prefers moderately fertile, dry, well-drained soil in full sun. The many selections include 'Blaufuchs' (syn. 'Blue Fox'), which has bright blue leaves. The blue-green leaves of 'Harz' are tipped purple.
Flowering height 30cm (12in)
Flowering time Summer (winter leaves)
Hardiness Fully hardy

Hakonechloa macra

This hardy Japanese grass is usually represented in gardens by the attractive cultivars 'Aureola', which has green-striped, yellow leaves, and 'Alboaurea' (syn. 'Variegata'), which has green, white and yellow leaves. The leaves of 'Aureola' are flushed with red in autumn. They are clump-forming plants, which make rounded cushions of tapering foliage. Small flowers are borne in spikelets in summer and early autumn, and these persist into winter. It prefers a moisture-retentive soil in shade or part shade. It is one of the most attractive and versatile ornamental grasses, and is suitable for growing in containers on patios, in courtyard gardens, rock gardens, or at the front of a mixed or herbaceous border.
Height 45cm (18in)
Flowering time Summer and autumn (winter leaves)
Hardiness Fully hardy

Imperata

The six species of grass in the genus are grown for the beauty of their leaves rather than for their flowers, which appear only in areas with long hot summers. They make a good foil to a range of flowering plants in mixed borders. Grow in any reasonable soil, preferably moisture-retentive, in sun or light shade. Remove the seed heads to prevent self-seeding (and reversion to plain green). Some winter protection – a dry mulch of straw, for instance – is advisable in very cold climates. *I. cylindrica* 'Rubra' (syn. 'Red Baron'), Japanese blood grass, is usually found in the form of this attractive cultivar, whose name refers to the red colouring that the leaves develop from the tip downwards.
Height 1m (3ft)
Flowering time Summer (winter leaves)
Hardiness Half-hardy

above left to right *Festuca glauca, Imperata cylindrica* 'Rubra' and *Hakonechloa macra* 'Alboaurea'.

below
Carex 'Frosted Curls'.

shrubs

An indispensable element of the winter garden, shrubs provide form, structure, fragrance and colour. A well-planted garden will have a selection of these useful plants, each contributing to the overall scheme. Topiarized evergreens and deciduous shrubs with scented winter flowers should be positioned where their characteristics can be appreciated to the full.

Chimonanthus

Commonly known as wintersweet, this is a genus of six species of evergreen and deciduous shrubs, although only one is widely grown and reliably hardy. Plant wintersweet where it will be hidden among summer-flowering shrubs.

below left to right An attractive dogwood by the edge of a pond, *Cornus alba* 'Sibirica', and *C. sanguinea* 'Winter Beauty'.

C. praecox

This deciduous shrub is grown for the intensely fragrant, bell-shaped yellow flowers, stained brownish-red inside, which are borne in midwinter on bare stems. In summer glossy, mid-green leaves, each to 20cm (8in) long, cover the stems. The cultivar 'Grandiflorus' has larger, deeper yellow flowers.

Flowering height 4m (12ft)
Flowering time Winter
Hardiness Fully hardy

Cornus

The dogwoods include some enormous trees, for which you will need a large garden, but there are some shrubs, which can be kept small by coppicing them every year. This forces them to put up a number of short stems, about 3m (10ft) high, the best of which are richly coloured. The spring coppicing can either involve cutting back every single stem, or just half so that it always has some growth. The two species to look for are *C. alba* and *C. sanguinea* and their cultivars.

Height 3m (10ft)
Flowering time Late spring and early summer (coloured winter stems)
Hardiness Fully hardy

Cotoneaster

Grow cotoneasters to provide a show of berries from autumn into winter, which range in colour from bright, shiny red (*C. adpressus, C. salicifolius* 'Herbstfeur' and *C. conspicuus*) to flashy yellow (*C. frigidus* 'Fructu Luteo'). One of the best is *C. horizontalis* with its spreading, horizontal branches, and the red berries clearly hung along them. They come in all sizes, from tiny shrubs to large trees. You can use the smallest in rockeries, to edge paths or beds and you will get, with the right choice, evergreen leaves, typically white or pink flowers (the earliest appearing in spring), and best of all, the berries. Tiny *C. procumbens* practically hugs the ground, *C. adpressus* 'Little Gem' is about 5cm (2in) high, and *C. dammeri* is 15cm (6in) high. *C. astrophoros* is slightly taller at 45cm (18in) and spreads 60–90cm (2–3ft), but takes about 30 years to do so. Good choices for hedges include the red-fruiting *C. glacialis*, *C. turbinatus* and *C. lacteus*. They can be pruned, and the show of flowers and berries will not suffer.

Height To 5m (15ft)

Flowering time Spring to summer (autumn and winter berries)

Hardiness Fully hardy

Daphne

Evergreen, semi-evergreen or deciduous, these delightful shrubs bear flowers with an exquisite fragrance. Some are rock garden plants, others work well in mixed or shrub borders. Winter-flowering types are best sited near a door where their fragrance can be appreciated to the full without the need to go too far outdoors. *D. bholua* is a borderline hardy, semi-evergreen species that bears deliciously scented clusters of pink and white flowers in late winter. The deciduous and hardiest variety *D. bholua* var. *glacialis* 'Gurkha' bears purplish-pink flowers from mid- to late winter. 'Jacqueline Postill' is evergreen, borderline hardy and has deep purplish-pink flowers. *D. mezereum* is a deciduous species, which suits a woodland garden, and produces reddish, highly scented flowers in late winter. The red summer berries are poisonous, but attractive. *D. tangutica* is a small, evergreen species originating from western China. The fragrant white flowers, which are tinged with rose-purple, appear in late winter to early spring.

Flowering height 60cm–3m (2–10ft)

Flowering time Winter and spring

Hardiness Half-hardy to fully hardy

above left to right *Daphne bholua*, the pretty yellow and dark pink flowers of *Chimonanthus praecox*, and *D. bholua* 'Jacqueline Postill'.

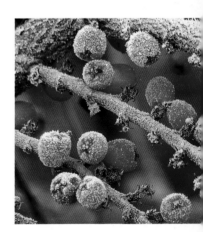

above The bright red berries of *Cotoneaster frigidus* 'Cornubia'.

Erica x darleyensis

Often known as Darley heath, or Darley Dale heath, *Erica x darleyensis* has many easy-to-grow hybrids with coloured young foliage and a long flowering period, usually from midwinter (sometimes earlier) until well into spring. The following selection of cultivars are all hardy. 'Archie Graham' has lilac-pink flowers. 'Arthur Johnson' (syn. 'Dunwood Splendour') has pink flowers, which deepen to lilac-pink, and foliage tipped with cream in spring. 'Jack H. Brummage' has lilac-pink flowers and foliage that is yellow-orange throughout the year. 'Jenny Porter' has pinkish-white flowers and cream-tipped foliage. 'Kramer's Rote' has magenta flowers and bronze-tinged foliage. 'Silberschmelze' (syn. 'Molten Silver') has ash-white flowers and foliage faintly tipped with cream in spring. 'White Perfection' has pure white flowers. Unlike most heathers, the Darley heath will tolerate alkaline soil, as long as it is free-draining, and in an open sunny position. By grouping a number of different coloured forms together you can create an effect similar to a multi-coloured patchwork quilt. This is invariably far more interesting and effective than when one or two ericas are grown alone. To add extra height, and prevent the look being too uniform, plant a couple of tall, narrow vertical conifers.

Flowering height To 60cm (24in)
Flowering time Winter to early spring
Hardiness Fully hardy

Garrya elliptica

It makes a remarkably indestructible and attractive evergreen shrub on free-draining soil. It is at its best from midwinter to early spring when it is covered by a mass of dangling grey-green catkins, 15–20cm (6–8in) long. If you want even longer catkins, choose 'James Roof'. *Garrya elliptica* can also be grown as a dense bushy hedge, but should only be pruned and kept in shape once the display of catkins has finished. It grows well in seaside gardens, but does not make a windbreak because it needs a sheltered position. When exposed to a flaying wind, it suffers badly.
Flowering height 4m (12ft)
Flowering time Midwinter to early spring
Hardiness Frost hardy

Hamamelis

The witch hazel genus contains some of the finest winter-flowering shrubs, which would no doubt be more widely grown were it not for their specific cultivation needs. Propagation is also difficult, and plants are slow-growing, so those offered for sale

tend to be small and expensive. Besides their spidery, scented winter flowers, they also have outstanding autumn and winter leaf colour. *H.* x *intermedia* is a group of variable hybrids. Selections include 'Arnold Promise', which has bright yellow winter flowers and splendid autumn leaf colour; 'Diane' which has red flowers and rich autumn tints; and the rare 'Vesna' with pale copper-coloured flowers and superb autumn leaf colour. *H. mollis*, Chinese witch hazel, is one of the best of the witch hazels. This slow-growing species has scented yellow flowers in midwinter.

Flowering height 4m (12ft)
Flowering time Winter
Hardiness Fully hardy

Jasminum nudiflorum

The winter jasmine has no scent, although the brilliant yellow flowers are undoubtedly welcome in the depths of winter. Not strictly climbing, the stems of this Chinese species are lax and trailing. It can be trained against a wall or allowed to cascade down a bank. The cheery, bright yellow flowers open during warm spells on the bare branches over winter.

Height 2m (7ft) or more
Flowering time Winter and early spring
Hardiness Fully hardy

above left to right
Hamamelis mollis 'Pallida', *Jasminum nudiflorum,* and *H. mollis* 'Pallida' with flowering *Erica carnea* 'Springwood White'.

left Catkins of *Garrya elliptica* in the snow.

above A brightly variegated holly adding extra flashes of colour.

opposite top left to bottom right *Ilex* x *aquipernyi* 'Dragon Lady', *Ilex aquifolium* 'Rubricaulis Aurea', *Lonicera fragrantissima* and *I. aquifolium* 'Harpune'.

Ilex

Hollies are essential in the winter garden. They have three important features. First, the often glossy foliage, sometimes variegated as in the case of *I. aquifolium* 'Argentea Marginata Pendula', *I. aquifolium* 'Golden van Tol' and *I. a.* 'Silver Queen'. The leaves really stand out in the depths of winter, especially when the variegation is bright yellow, as with 'Golden van Tol'. Second, most hollies can be topiarized. Their leaves are quite large so it is hard to convert them into tight-angled shapes, but they will make good lollipops. And third, many have an excellent display of red and yellow berries over winter. Note that if you do want berries you must grow a male and a female in close proximity and check carefully before you buy.

I. x altaclerensis

The Highclere holly is fast-growing and can be clipped to create a hedge, although left unpruned it will make an upright tree, to 20m (65ft) tall. Several attractive cultivars have been developed. The heights and spread vary according to how regularly and closely plants are pruned. 'Belgica Aurea', a compact female form, has leaves that are irregularly edged with yellow; 'Cameliifolia', a female form, which is good for hedging, has glossy, dark green leaves that have smooth edges and turn bronze in cold weather and scarlet berries; 'Golden King', a compact female form, has gold-edged leaves and red berries; 'Lawsoniana', a compact female form, has green leaves with yellow-splashed centres and red berries; and 'Wilsonii', a vigorous female form, has bright green leaves and many bright red berries.
Flowering height To 20m (65ft)
Flowering time Winter berries
Hardiness Fully hardy

I. aquifolium

The common or English holly will also make an upright, large tree if left unchecked, but plants can be pruned and clipped to keep them within bounds.

Some of the cultivars that have been developed have strikingly variegated foliage. 'Argentea Marginata Pendula' (syn. 'Argentea Pendula'), a female form, has cream-edged leaves, purplish stems and red berries; 'Ferox Argentea' (silver hedgehog holly), a slow-growing male form, has sharply spiny, cream-edged leaves; 'Golden Queen' (syn. 'Aurea Regina'), a male form, has spiny, gold-edged leaves; 'Handsworth New Silver', a female form, has purple stems, spiny, cream-edged leaves and bright red berries; 'J.C. van Tol', a self-fertile, female form, has dark green leaves with very few spines and dark red berries; and 'Silver Queen' (syn. 'Silver King'), a slow-growing male form, has cream-edged, spiny leaves.
Flowering height 20m (65ft)
Flowering time Winter berries
Hardiness Fully hardy

I. crenata

The Japanese or box-leaved holly has small, dark green, glossy leaves. It can be clipped to form good topiary shapes and produces black or, sometimes, white or yellow berries. 'Golden Gem', a spreading, compact, female form, has yellow-flecked leaves and black berries.
Flowering height 5m (15ft)
Flowering time Winter berries
Hardiness Fully hardy

Lonicera fragrantissima

A good plant for winter interest, this deciduous or semi-evergreen Chinese honeysuckle species has small, fragrant, white and pink flowers in midwinter. It keeps flowering from the time the leaves fall in autumn until early spring. Unfortunately, it is rather dull the rest of the time, unless used as a support for annual climbers, such as sweet peas. Nonetheless, it is a vital plant for winter gardens.
Flowering height 1.5m (5ft)
Flowering time Winter and early spring
Hardiness Fully hardy

above *Viburnum x bodnantense.*

below left to right
Mahonia trifolia, M. x *media* 'Buckland' in full flower, and *M. x media* 'Lionel Fortescue'.

Mahonia

The genus contains about 70 species of evergreen shrubs, which are rather similar to *Berberis* – in fact, some botanists would like to unite the genera. Most have deliciously scented flowers, but their prime use is to fill inhospitable sites.

M. aquifolium

Mountain grape holly or Oregon grape, as it is commonly known, has glossy green leaves and racemes of yellow flowers in late winter to early spring. There are a number of cultivars, including the vigorous and low-growing 'Apollo', and 'Smaragd', which has bronze, netted foliage.
Flowering height 1m (3ft)
Flowering time Late winter and spring
Hardiness Fully hardy

M. japonica

This erect species produces arching racemes of scented yellow flowers from early winter to early spring, followed by blue-purple berries. The selection 'Bealei' has more compact flower spikes.
Flowering height 2m (7ft)
Flowering time Winter to spring
Hardiness Fully hardy

M. lomariifolia

This elegant species is one of the parents of *M. x media* (the other is *M. japonica*), which it resembles in some respects, though it is more rangy in habit and slightly less resistant to extreme cold. The racemes of flowers, which smell like lily-of-the-valley, appear from late autumn to winter and are followed by bluish, grape-like fruits.
Flowering height 3m (10ft)
Flowering time Late autumn to winter
Hardiness Fully hardy

M. x media

This hybrid group includes a number of notable named garden selections, all similar and equally effective and all with long racemes of fragrant yellow flowers in winter. Leggy specimens can be pruned hard in spring. They include 'Charity', which has slender, upright, spreading spikes of very fragrant yellow flowers; 'Lionel Fortescue', which has upright plumes of bright yellow, slightly less fragrant flowers; and 'Winter Sun', which has dense clusters of bright yellow flowers.
Flowering height To 5m (15ft)
Flowering time Late autumn to late winter
Hardiness Fully hardy

M. trifolia

This unusual species is variable, existing in both prostrate and more upright forms. The short spikes of yellow flowers appear in spring, and the leaves flush purple-red in cold weather.

Flowering height 2m (7ft)
Flowering time Late winter and spring
Hardiness Fully hardy

Sarcococca

Christmas box, or sweet box, are excellent plants for the winter garden and have small but highly scented flowers among the shiny evergreen leaves. Use them with snowdrops, *Arum italicum* subsp. *italicum* 'Marmoratun' and early hellebores. They make excellent groundcover under deciduous trees, and flowering stems can be cut for use in winter flower arrangements. *S. confusa* is a low-growing shrub with glossy, dark green leaves. In winter it produces clusters of fragrant white flowers, and these are followed by glossy black fruits. The naturally occurring variety *S. hookeriana* var. *digyna*, the most widely grown form, has equally fragrant white flowers with pink sepals in mid- to late winter and blackish-blue fruit. *S. humilis* is a dwarf shrub, bearing pink-tinged, white flowers and blackish-blue fruit.

Flowering height To 1.5m (5ft)
Flowering time Winter
Hardiness Fully hardy

Viburnum

This large and important genus consists of both evergreen and deciduous shrubs that, between them, provide interest throughout the year. Some are grown for their flowers (winter or spring), others for their berries, and some for both. They are essential plants. Native species are excellent in wild gardens, providing food for birds in winter. Others are good in winter gardens or mixed borders. A select few make good specimens. *V. tinus*, which can be trained as a standard, is an important evergreen winter shrub. It has a rounded habit and white flowers in late winter or early spring. Bluish-black berries follow the flowers. The flowers of the popular cultivar 'Eve Price' open from rich eye-catching pink buds. *V. x bodnantense* 'Dawn' is one of the stars of the winter garden. It is a highly desirable upright, deciduous, vase-shaped shrub with richly scented, pink flowers opening in mild spells from autumn to spring. *V. plicatum* f. *tomentosum* produces blue-black berries in autumn and winter as the leaves redden. *V. farreri* (syn. *V. fragrans*) is deciduous, but it provides a major attraction in late autumn and early winter with its pretty, scented white flowers. The flowers are followed by a good show of tiny, round bright berries. It grows to a height of about 3m (10ft).

Flowering height To 3m (10ft)
Flowering time Late autumn to spring
Hardiness Fully hardy

above left to right
Vibernum tinus 'Eve Price',
Sarcococca confusa and
Viburnum plicatum 'Mariesii'.

below *Viburnum tinus* 'Gwenllian'.

above left to right
Betula utilis var. *jacquemontii,*
the bark of *B. utilis* var.
jacquemontii, and *Betula*
with an underplanting
of *Cornus.*

trees

The forms of trees are seen at their best in winter when many perennials and bulbs are taking a rest. They come in all shapes and sizes, from the pencil-thin, which shoot straight up, to giants for large gardens. The best have coloured bark, ranging from white to shiny brown, from green to a marbling of white with grey and fawn. Some have twisty, curly stems, which form patterns against the sky. There are also plenty of trees for medium-sized gardens, many offering an excellent show of autumn and winter berries.

Betula

Birches are among the best garden trees. They are hardy and easy to grow in addition to being graceful and quick growing. Most have attractive, usually white bark and good autumn leaf colour. They are among the most reliable trees for alkaline soils. *B. utilis* var. *jacquemontii* is a naturally occurring variety of the Himalayan birch, which has white bark, making it an outstanding plant for the winter garden. The oval leaves turn yellow in autumn. Many of the plants sold in the trade under this name are raised from seed collected in the Himalayas, so habits and growth rates can vary, but most will not exceed a height of 12m (40ft) in 20 years. Selected seedlings include 'Grayswood Ghost', which has glossy leaves; the fast-growing 'Jermyns', which has rounded leaves and large catkins (pussy willows); and 'Silver Shadow', which has large, drooping, dark green leaves. All three forms have particularly brilliant bark.

Height To 25m (82ft)

Flowering time Spring (autumn foliage, winter bark)

Hardiness Fully hardy

Corylus

Hazels provide long, dangly yellow catkins from late winter to early spring. The best form of hazel to buy is undoubtedly *C. avellana* 'Contorta', known as the corkscrew hazel or sometimes called Harry Lauder's walking stick. What makes it so special is the array of zig-zagging, twisty stems that really stand out in the winter, after the leaves have dropped. The stems can be used in cut flower displays. When you cut several stems for an indoor flower arrangement, hammer the stems well before giving them a long drink. As well as their striking stems, they have a fantastic array of twisty, thin, corkscrewing bare branches. They make a lively architectural tracery against the sky. *Corylus* grows well in most soils but they must be free-draining and fertile. A pruning regime is not necessary, but if you want to thin out the tangle of stems or prune to restrict size, do so over winter from the end of autumn to the start of spring.

Height 5m (15ft)
Flowering time Late winter
Hardiness Fully hardy

Eucalyptus

A familiar sight in many urban areas, eucalyptus trees are often planted as pollution-tolerant street trees. Not all species are fully hardy. Although potentially very large, they respond well to pruning. The foliage of most species changes shape as the tree matures, the juvenile leaves being generally considered the more attractive. Cutting back stems or pollarding regularly ensures that trees retain their youthful appearance. *E. pauciflora* subsp. *niphophila*, commonly known as snow gum or alpine snow gum, is a slow-growing evergreen tree, grown for its brilliant, peeling, cream and grey bark. It is shown to best advantage when the plant is grown as a multi-stemmed tree. The bluish-grey juvenile leaves are oval; adult leaves are sickle-shaped. It is hardier than many types of eucalyptus and will grow in any well-drained soil in full sun. It has the most beautiful bark, and is well worth growing.

Height 6m (20ft) or more
Flowering time Late spring to summer (winter bark)
Hardiness Fully hardy to frost tender

below left to right
Corylus avellana 'Contorta',
C. avellana with catkins
in winter and *Eucalyptus
pauciflora* subsp. *niphophila*.

Prunus

The ornamental cherries are usually regarded as spring-flowering species, but there are two trees that ought to be in every winter garden. They are *P. serrula* and *P.* x *subhirtella* 'Autumnalis'. The former offers striking, shiny bark, with white flowers in the spring making a beautiful combination, followed by fruit resembling cherries. The latter has an intermittent show of flowers, which starts in the autumn. They are not big but they are abundant.

below left to right

There is room for the shiny, brown-stemmed *Prunus serrula* even in medium-sized gardens – grow it as a feature plant where it can be clearly seen; *Prunus serrula* planted with *Viburnum tinus,* and *Prunus* x *subhirtella* 'Autumnalis'.

P. serrula

A Tibetan cherry tree from western China, this is usually planted for its gleaming, mahogany-red bark, which peels off in strips to produce an eye-catching feature in winter. Site it where the tree will be well lit by the winter sun.

Height 10m (33ft)
Flowering time Spring (winter bark)
Hardiness Fully hardy

P. x subhirtella 'Autumnalis'

The autumn cherry, which was developed in Japan, is probably the finest winter-flowering tree, producing flushes of pink-tinged, white flowers throughout winter during mild spells. The peak display usually occurs right at the end of winter, shortly before the equinox. The leaves turn yellow in autumn.

Height 8m (25ft)
Flowering time Winter
Hardiness Fully hardy

Stewartia pseudocamellia

The peeling pink to red-brown and grey bark of this deciduous tree is a distinctive feature in the winter. The finely toothed, dark green leaves turn yellow to orange to red during the autumn. Cup-shaped, white flowers are borne singly or in pairs in midsummer.

Height 20m (65ft)
Flowering time Midsummer (winter bark)
Hardiness Fully hardy

Salix

The willow genus contains creeping shrubs as well as some quite large trees. Willows offer a variety of attractions for the garden. Many are grown for their catkins (pussy willows) or brightly coloured young shoots – regular annual or biennial hard pruning ensures a good supply – and weeping varieties look attractive growing at the water's edge. *S. babylonica* var. *pekinensis* 'Tortuosa' is a bizarre tree almost grown exclusively for the interest of its twisted stems, at their most striking in winter. *S. caprea* 'Kilmarnock' is a weeping miniature, with cascades of silver-white catkins in late winter. The tree is created artificially by grafting a prostrate plant on to rootstocks of varying height. *S.* x *sepulcralis* var. *chrysocoma* is a fast-growing golden weeping willow that is possibly the most familiar of all willows. It is an evocative sight when the tips of its arching branches trail in water. It is equally attractive when bare in winter as when it is clothed in its bright green, lance-shaped leaves in summer.

Height To 15m (50ft)
Flowering time Spring (winter stems)
Hardiness Fully hardy

Tilia

Many forms of lime tree make excellent garden plants. Pollard or pleach them to restrict their size, albeit at the expense of the flowers. Lime trees will grow in any moderately fertile, well-drained soil (preferably alkaline), in sun or light shade. *T. cordata*, small-leaved lime, is an upright European species that flowers in midsummer; the heart-shaped leaves turn yellow in autumn. *T. c.* 'Winter Orange' is a desirable selection, with golden-orange young stems that are a feature in winter. Cut back hard for the best winter display. The leaves of *T. platyphyllus* 'Rubra' turn yellow in autumn, and shoots are red in winter.

Height 25m (82ft) (unpollarded)
Flowering time Midsummer (winter stems)
Hardiness Fully hardy

below left to right
The bark of *Stewartia pseudocamellia* in winter, *Tilia platyphyllus*, and *Salix babylonica* var. *pekinensis* 'Tortuosa'.

above *Abies procera.*

below left to right *Abies cephalonica,* cones of *A. koreana* and *A. amabilis.*

conifers

Conifers offer a fantastic range of colours and shapes, from giant specimens like the Leyland cypress to prostrate dwarfs that hug the ground. There are hundreds to choose from. Most are evergreen, and they inject an enormous amount of interest to the winter garden. By themselves some might not look spectacular, but they come into their own when they are planted as focal points, in combination with each other or in association with winter-flowering heathers. For the best range, visit a nursery specializing in conifers.

Abies

Silver firs are found throughout Europe, North Africa, Asia and North America, especially in mountainous areas. Many grow too large for the average garden, but there are some dwarf and slow-growing forms. The compact forms can be planted in borders and rock gardens, although some of the larger species look best when grown as feature plants. Most silver firs are conical and all are evergreen. Grow them in well-drained, slightly acid soil.

A. amabilis

The Pacific silver fir is not widely grown, but the selection 'Spreading Star' makes excellent groundcover. The glossy, dark green needles smell of oranges when they are crushed, and the cones are deep purple.
Height 50cm (20in)
Hardiness Fully hardy

A. balsamea

Balsam fir, or balm of Gilead, is unfamiliar in gardens, but it has a number of notable cultivars. All are hardy. Those classified as Hudsonia Group are dwarf trees, usually compact and rounded in form, although there is some variation. 'Nana', a good rock garden conifer, makes a dome-shaped bush, which is tolerant of some shade. The aromatic, shiny green, needle-like leaves, shorter than those on the species, are arranged in two ranks on the stems; the cones are purplish-blue.
Height To 15m (50ft)
Hardiness Fully hardy

A. cephalonica

Greek fir is a rare tree and, at 30m (100ft) in height, it is unsuitable for small gardens, but the selection

'Meyer's Dwarf' (syn. 'Nana') is more manageable at a height of 50cm (20in), forming a low, spreading, flat-topped, shade-tolerant mound that is good in a rock garden. The needle-like leaves are glossy green and are shorter than on the species; the cones are greenish-brown and resinous.
Height To 30m (100ft)
Hardiness Fully hardy

A. koreana
Korean fir is one of the most attractive of the silver firs. It is notable for its impressive violet cones, which age to brown. The needles are dark green.
Height 10m (33ft)
Hardiness Fully hardy

A. procera
Noble fir (syn. *A. nobilis*), from the western United States, forms a cone-shaped tree, which matures to a broader, irregular obelisk. The greyish-green needles, sometimes with a bluish cast, are arranged in two ranks. Mature trees have silvery-grey, fissured bark; the cones are green. The noble fir makes an attractive specimen, particularly when young; it is sometimes used as a Christmas tree. It is wind-tolerant and reliable at high altitudes.
Height To 45m (150ft)
Hardiness Fully hardy

Cedrus
This is a small genus of only four species, but arguably it contains the most magnificent of all conifers when mature. They are generally suitable only for large gardens, but they are worth considering if you are prepared to remove them once they start to get too large. They make ideal lawn specimens if they can be allowed the space to grow to maturity.

C. atlantica
Originating from the Atlas Mountains in North Africa, this species is less common in gardens than some of the following selections. 'Aurea' has bright, golden-yellow leaves. *C. atlantica* f. *glauca* ('Blue Atlas' cedar) is one of the most handsome forms. Initially cone-shaped, it develops a more spreading crown. The needles, white when young but becoming bright glaucous blue, are arranged in clusters; the cones are light green. Plants in cultivation are normally sold under the name Glauca Group (indicating that they may vary). 'Glauca Pendula', also glaucous blue, has an arching leader and pendulous branches, and it develops as a tent-like structure. It can be kept small by cutting back the central leader, which will persuade the horizontal branches to spread more widely (they may need support as a result).
Height 40m (130ft)
Hardiness Fully hardy

above left to right *Cedrus atlantica* 'Aurea', *C. atlantica* 'Glauca Pendula', and *C. a.* f. *glauca* 'Blue Atlas'.

below
Abies balsamea 'Nana'.

Chamaecyparis

False cypress is a useful genus, from East Asia and North America, with a huge number of cultivars. They range from giant forest trees to smaller forms that can be used as specimen trees, for hedging and as dwarf plants for the rock or scree garden.

C. lawsoniana

Lawson cypress (syn. *Cupressus lawsoniana*), a conical tree, native to North America, is too large for many gardens, but it has given rise to many cultivars of widely diverging habits. All are hardy. Among the best dwarfs is 'Aurea Densa', which is rounded and one of the outstanding golden-leaved cultivars. It grows to 2m (7ft). The slow-growing 'Bleu Nantais' is another good blue-green, making a cone-shaped mound, about 1.5m (5ft) high. Both have needle-like leaves that become scale-like. Taller varieties include the conical 'Ellwoodii', which is one of the most popular grey-green varieties. The weeping 'Pembury Blue' has striking bluish-grey foliage.
Height To 15m (50ft)
Hardiness Fully hardy

C. obtusa

Hinoki cypress (syn. *Cupressus obtusa*) is less tolerant of lime than some species, and it is not widely planted, yielding to its many cultivars. 'Crippsii' (syn. 'Crippsii Aurea') is a rich gold when grown in full sun, making a fine specimen reaching 15m (50ft). 'Nana Gracilis' is a dwarf cultivar, forming a rough pyramid.
Height To 20m (65ft)
Hardiness Fully hardy

x Cupressocyparis

The value of this much maligned hybrid genus between *Chamaecyparis nootkatensis* and *Cupressus macrocarpa* lies in the trees' speed of growth. It is often planted as hedging where a pollution-resistant screen is needed quickly, and it makes a tough, tight hedge, but only if cut regularly. Allowed to grow freely, it gets out of hand.

x Cupressocyparis leylandii

Leyland cypress is the hybrid mostly used for hedging. All are hardy. 'Golconda', one of the most decorative, forms a narrow cone shape. The scale-like leaves, carried in flattened sprays, are brilliant golden-yellow; the cones are rounded. It is tolerant of clipping. 'Leighton Green' develops as a tall, cone-shaped tree with bright green foliage.
Height To 35m (115ft)
Hardiness Fully hardy

Cupressus

Cypress trees are characteristic of the Mediterranean and are among the stateliest of conifers. They are not always easy to grow away from their native habitat, but they can be used as fine specimens or for hedging. They resent transplanting, so always look for young specimens rather than mature trees.

C. arizonica var. glabra

Smooth cypress (syn. *C. glabra*), which is native to the South-western United States, is a good specimen where space is limited. It forms a regular cone shape. On young specimens the bark is smooth, reddish-purple and flaking; it thickens and turns to greyish-brown on older trees. The scale-like leaves are glaucous bluish-grey and aromatic; the cones are dark brown.
Height To 15m (50ft)
Hardiness Fully hardy

C. macrocarpa

Monterey cypress was once widely used for hedging, but it has largely been superseded by x *Cupressocyparis leylandii*. Excellent cultivars have been developed from the species, however. Both those listed here are borderline hardy. 'Donard Gold' forms an elegant obelisk that gradually becomes conical. The bright yellowish-green leaves are aromatic when crushed. 'Goldcrest' is a desirable smaller version.
Height To 30m (100ft)
Hardiness Mostly fully hardy

opposite top row left to right x *Cupressocyparis leylandii* 'Leighton Green', x *C. leylandii* 'Golconda' and *Cupressus arizonica* var. *glabra*, **middle row** *Chamaecyparis lawsoniana* 'Bleu Nantais', *Cupressus arizonica* var. *glabra* 'Blue Ice' and *Chamaecyparis pisifera* 'Filifera Aurea', **bottom row** *Cupressus macrocarpa* 'Donard Gold', *Chamaecyparis lawsoniana* 'Aurea Densa' and *Chamaecyparis obtusa* 'Nana Gracilis'.

above Winter berries on a juniper tree.

below left to right
Juniperus communis 'Hibernica', *Pinus sylvestris* and *Juniperus chinensis* 'Aurea'.

Juniperus

Junipers are usually represented in gardens by the cultivars and hybrids rather than by the species. Many are rock garden plants, while others look good grouped in island beds. They also do well in troughs and containers. Female plants bear berry-like fruits, which may be used to flavour game dishes.

J. chinensis

Chinese juniper is not notable in itself, but it has given rise to many attractive cultivars. 'Aurea' (Young's golden juniper), a slow-growing male selection that forms a narrow obelisk, has aromatic, dull golden-yellow leaves, which are wedge-shaped initially but become scale-like as they mature. Many cones appear in spring, and the tree produces its best colour in sun.
Height To 20m (65ft)
Hardiness Fully hardy

J. communis

Common juniper is found throughout the northern hemisphere. Selections include 'Hibernica' (Irish juniper), which makes a distinctive, narrow shrub, the foliage having a bluish-green cast. The range of cultivars also includes the dwarf, slow-growing kind, though they will eventually, after many years, reach 9m (30ft). Note that some plants are male and some female. The latter are well worth growing because they have round green berries with a greyish tinge, which eventually end up black, though this takes from two to three years.
Height 3–5m (10–15ft)
Hardiness Fully hardy

J. horizontalis

Creeping juniper is a ground-hugging conifer from North America. The species forms a mat of greyish-green leaves, which are needle-like when young, becoming scale-like with age, with dark blue berries. There are many attractive cultivars, all suitable for groundcover. 'Blue Chip' (syn. 'Blue Moon') has glaucous blue foliage. 'Douglasii' is bluish-green, turning rich purple in autumn. 'Golden Carpet' is bright yellowish-green.
Height To 30cm (12in)
Hardiness Fully hardy

Picea

Spruces are found throughout the northern hemisphere and are widely planted as Christmas trees, *P. abies* being the usual choice. There is a wide range of garden varieties, some with grey, yellow or blue foliage. Most are symmetrical in shape, and there are many dwarf forms suitable for rock gardens.

P. abies

The Norway spruce is native to Scandinavia, and is a conical tree. It is the traditional choice for Christmas trees in Europe. 'Gregoryana' is an attractive dwarf selection that makes an impenetrable mound of dark green foliage. It is one of the most compact of all dwarf conifers, growing to about 60cm (2ft).
Height To 40m (130ft)
Hardiness Fully hardy

P. pungens

The Colorado spruce is the parent of many notable garden plants. 'Globosa', which forms a neat dome or mound, has bristle-like, glaucous green foliage, arranged radially. 'Montgomery' is silver-blue, making a broad-based cone. Slow-growing, it should be among the first choices for a specimen tree in a small garden.
Height To 15m (50ft)
Hardiness Fully hardy

Pinus

Most pines, such as *Pinus sylvestris*, are unsuitable as garden plants, magnificent though they are, since they are nearly all too large for the average plot. Selection by nurserymen has produced a number of useful clones that are more manageable, however. The needles, which are sometimes quite long, are held in characteristic bundles.

P. mugo

Dwarf mountain pine is a useful conifer from central Europe that is less widely grown than its many garden-worthy clones, many of them dwarf and ideal for a rock garden. 'Corley's Mat' makes a prostrate, spreading carpet. The slow-growing 'Mops' is almost spherical with resinous brown buds in winter.
Height 3.5m (11ft)
Hardiness Fully hardy

above A close-up of the bright blue-tinged needles of *Picea pungens* 'Hoopsii'.

below left to right
Picea pungens 'Montgomery', *Pinus mugo* 'Corley's Mat' and *Picea abies* 'Gregoryana'.

WINTER DISPLAYS

Planning a garden that looks attractive and interesting in winter requires some thought. There are plenty of plants that will provide colour, form and fragrance in the winter garden, but it is important to integrate these with the other plants that are grown primarily for their appearance in spring and summer. The winter garden also depends to a large extent on the underlying structure and design for its effect. The bare bones of the hard landscaping and boundaries are more noticeable in winter, and all planting must be planned to enhance the built features when they are most exposed.

left *Galanthus* 'Magnet' has taller, larger flowers than *Galanthus nivalis* (common snowdrop). Here, it forms a marvellous carpet beneath the witch hazel *Hamamelis* x *intermedia* 'Pallida'.

carpets of colour

The best way to make sure that the winter garden looks good is to work in layers from the bottom up. Start off with small plants that hug the ground, then make sure you have interesting shapes in beds and borders over the winter months, before moving on to topiary, trees, conifers, and artificial shapes.

winter bulbs

Many people think that the only bulbs worth planting are those that flower in spring, yet there are some sensational ones for the winter. These will brighten up a woodland garden or a patch of ground beneath a deciduous tree. This is an ideal place for planting because the bare branches mean that bright light reaches the ground in winter, when the bulbs need it

above A beautiful mix of purple-pink cyclamens in the foregound, setting off bright yellow and deep, rich mauve crocuses.

right A clever mix of bright yellow *Eranthis hyemalis* (winter aconite), with a great leafy mound of a *Helleborus foetidus* (stinking hellebore) behind.

most. The trees are also dormant now, taking up less moisture from the ground. Conversely, in summer, when the bulbs are taking a rest and not needing too much moisture, the trees are in full growth. The two make a perfect combination.

The pick of the bulbs includes *Cyclamen coum, Eranthis hyemalis* (winter aconite) and *Galanthus* (snowdrop). Cyclamen should be planted in big, bold groups for the best effect. Because they are so small, just 5–7.5cm (2–3in) high, a single plant can easily get lost, but together their beautifully patterned leaves really stand out. Some are completely green and some have silver marbling. Their shapes vary from round to kidney-shaped. In the wild they grow in shady mountain sites, invariably with good drainage, and the two key qualities they need in the garden are summer shade and gritty, free-draining soil. In the right conditions just a few plants will eventually create a wonderful spread.

Winter aconites also do best in open areas under deciduous trees as long as they are well watered (it is vital that they do not bake in the summer). In a mild winter they might start flowering quite early, but generally it takes a good while before the flashy spreads of bright yellow flowers appear. The latter open only in full sun and will not perform in the shade, so do not hide them away. In very bad winters they might not flower until the first days of spring, but the wait is well worth it, especially after a couple of years of planting when they have self-seeded and created an eye-catching show.

Snowdrops are equally showy. There are many kinds with minuscule differences. Choose a sturdy, strong growing cultivar, such as the scented 'S. Arnott' or 'Atkinsii'. They need winter moisture and summer shade so that they do not bake. They soon spread, making great swathes of white. Some make lovely cut flowers for any indoor display.

above Pretty snowdrops always provide a bright white show.

below The best place to grow *Cyclamen coum* is around the base of a large, deciduous tree.

borders

Before you dig a new border, it is vital that you first
decide what its outline will look like in winter, when it
is clearly visible and most of the plants are taking a
rest. Walk around the garden, getting different views,
and decide whether you need a circular shape, a
smart triangle, a series of beds with paths weaving
between them, or a single, impressive island bed.

It is also important to decide how you are going
to edge it. To make the border stand out, you could
use treated posts, sawn into lengths, to give the edges
a distinctive, rustic look. Alternatively, use brick or if it
is a large bed, paving. Make sure that the soil is not
completely bare from winter to spring. And odd
though it sounds, it does not matter if the growth is
alive or dead.

Ornamental grasses are excellent value for money.
They provide fresh green spring growth, summer
flowers and sometimes reddish-orange autumn

colour. It can be very tempting to cut down the dead
stems at the start of winter, but do not do so. Leave
them. They look especially attractive when rimed
with winter frost. They also provide interesting shapes
and seedheads. The best time to cut them down is in
late winter, before the new spring growth begins.

pampas grass and evergreens

Some of the most sensational ornamental grasses
include the pampas grasses. They can grow 3m (10ft)
high in the case of the popular *Cortaderia selloana*,
which has several, excellent cultivars. 'Sunningdale
Silver' has strong, vertical flowering stems, topped by
beautiful, silvery-creamy-white plumes. Leave them
standing over winter, and the winter garden will be
immeasurably enhanced. Structural seedheads left
uncut over winter can look stunning in wintry frosts.

There are several low-growing conifers that can
be used to provide year-round groundcover, but do
not overlook *Hedera* spp. (ivy), which are available in a

wide range of leaf colour and shape and which can be easily kept under control by simply pulling up straggling stems. In reliably moist soil and shade the glossy, evergreen leaves of *Pachysandra terminalis* will quickly create a dense mat through which taller spring-flowering bulbs can emerge.

theatrical touches

You do not need a grand garden for a theatrical touch. A stylish flourish can perk up the smallest garden. Make sure that each effect is fully embellished. A statue by itself might be fine, but it will look even more effective against a background of winter evergreens. This can be anything from dwarf evergreen bamboos to smart shrubs and conifers. They will stand out even more beautifully and dramatically when the garden is covered in snow.

above A lively mix of shapes will keep the winter garden alive. Combine verticals (seedheads and trees) with strong horizontals (the hedge top and path running from left to right).

left A stylish feature such as a sundial will look equally attractive in winter and summer.

above Large topiary like this needs a spacious lawn, but the design can easily be scaled down for a more intimate setting.

below and right These well-established pieces of topiary create a wonderful sense of rhythm, leading on the eye to the end of the garden.

topiary

Topiary can be as traditional or as modern, as abstract or representational as you wish. All that counts is that you choose the right plant for cutting, pruning and shaping and that it fits in with the rest of the garden.

boxing clever

For traditional evergreen topiary use *Buxus* (box). It can be used to make all kinds of shapes, from squares to balls and peacocks. The small leaves mean you can create precise shapes with tight angles, and it is quite fast growing, at about 30cm (12in) a year. Box responds well to regular clipping.

You can buy box plants at various heights, some of which are already trained, although they are expensive. Alternatively, buy an unpruned box plant that is about three years old. Plant it where it is needed, and then take your time deciding what shape will look best. You can be as unconventional as you want, creating all kinds of intricate shapes, including cubes with a central stem poking out of the top,

trained into a globe, with a central stem poking out of that, and a small bird trained on top of that.

The simplest shapes are created by eye and require three things – a sharp pair of secateurs, a clear idea of what you want to achieve and a steady hand. If necessary, buy a ready-made, three-dimensional template to stand over the plant, or make a former yourself using chicken wire. It does not matter if the topiary is not exactly as you would wish because further snippings and growth will rectify any mistakes.

Do make sure that whatever you create has room to grow and fill out, with visitors given plenty of space to stand back and appreciate what you have done. Topiary never works when you are standing right on top of it, unable to see how it fits into the rest of the garden. It needs to be seen from a distance.

hedge topiary

The most formal, structural plants in the garden often make the best topiary, and that includes evergreen hedges. Too often they are left as sprawling, misshapen slabs around the garden, when they can so easily be turned into something elegant, beautiful and striking.

Box hedges can be given a battlemented look, a straight top or one with an array of shapes. They include balls and pyramids, at regular intervals, and merely require someone with a head for heights perched on a sturdy stepladder. Make sure that the shapes have sloping or rounded tops, so that snow can easily slide off. It is easy to swish snow off topiary in the garden so that the shapes do not get squashed, but at the top of a hedge that can be extremely tricky.

Other plants for topiary, besides box, include *Ilex* (holly), *Prunus lusitanica* (Portugal laurel) and *Taxus baccata* (common yew). You can also train *Hedera* spp. (ivy) over wire shapes for instant, easy topiary. Just shear all the leaves off one side so that you are faced with an attractive, twisty mass of short, bare stems. Right on top, and down the other side, will be a 7.5cm (3in) layer of leaves. This creates a thin curtain of foliage that filters the light.

The best way to start a beech hedge is by planting bare-root trees over winter, 15–30cm (6–12in) apart. Do this when the weather is clement. Let the beech reach its final height, say 2.5m (8ft), then prune the top growth in late autumn or early winter, as the sap levels fall. At the same time, shear the growth off one side. Old established hedges can be pruned over two or three years, to minimize the shock. Keep cutting off new growth on the bald side.

The effect is highly striking and unusual. It is not traditional topiary, but it is a clever way of manipulating growth to a stylish, surprising effect. The ultimate aim is to keep the winter garden alive, and flourishing. By injecting extra levels of interest, your winter garden will bring as much pleasure as it does in the summer.

above A double-topiary "look" with a pair of pyramids set in front of a topiarized hedge, complete with a door into the next part of the garden.

left A bold piece of shapely, striking topiary.

below Small parterres should be placed near a house, where they can be looked down upon.

tree schemes

The importance of trees in garden design can easily be overlooked. In summer they are part of the scene, making masses of leafy growth, but in winter, when the bare branches are revealed, they often have a majestic beauty.

Trees need to be looked after as much as small plants to give their best. The best trees have either coloured stems or create wonderful silhouettes against the light. Mature trees might well need thinning at some stage if they are to be effective. Lopping off branches lets light get to the ground, where there are bulbs, and also makes sure that the tree has an open, striking outline. It is also important to make sure that any twiggy growth sprouting out of the base of the trunk is removed, giving a clean look.

planting trees

When you are planting trees make sure that they fit in with the rest of the scheme. At ground level this might include a sensational spread of a white-flowering *Erica carnea* (winter heath), creating an effect like snow. To this, add rich, glossy, shiny greens, deep purples and variegated yellowish leaves. With just a few choice colours a large part of the garden can be given an astonishing make-over.

It is also important to make sure that trees are integrated by working down from (or up to) their great height. Provide adjacent hedges and shrubs, in different shapes and colours, so that each stratum is clearly visible. The bare-stemmed *Cornus alba* and *C. stolonifera*, and their different cultivars, add a range of blackish-purple, bright red and yellow-green vertical stems that strikingly reach for the sky.

There are also plenty of small trees for medium-sized gardens. The most important thing is that every plant has its own space, and that each ingredient blends without jarring.

opposite The winter garden scene with *Erica carnea* 'Springwood White' on the ground, and a magisterial tree showing where branches have been removed to open up its striking shape.

left The candelabra-effect of a *Prunus* tree set against pyramids and verticals.

below left A deft fusion of foreground green, middle-ground flame-red, and a background mix of the two.

below The coloured stems of a *Cornus* cleverly placed against a lilac background.

above A stylish conifer windbreak, using a row of giant hedges.

conifers

The most important point about a winter garden is that the design and the planting create a strong shape and structure. It is easy to pack a garden with summer-flowering plants, but a one-season wonder is no good whatsoever. Carefully selected and sited conifers are essential ingredients of the well-planned garden.

what do they do?

The best conifers add shapes and contours whether you want a formal or informal scheme. With heights ranging from 1m (3ft) for a dwarf conifer, such as *Picea pungens* 'Globosa', to the 90m (300ft) high *Sequoiadendron giganteum* (giant redwood), there is a conifer for most situations.

Conifers are best appreciated in winter, when the rest of the garden is relatively quiet. Many have decorative cones. Those of *Abies koreana* (Korean fir) are a striking violet-blue, while those of *Pinus peuce* (Macedonian pine) exude white resin. *Pinus bungeana* has decorative bark, richly deserving its common

right A beautifully subtle range of coloured conifers.

name, the lacebark pine. The bark flakes off to reveal creamy patches that darken to purplish grey-green. Some cultivars of *Cryptomeria japonica* (Japanese cedar) that retain their juvenile foliage redden dramatically in winter. And the blue-green leaved conifers are a boon to winter gardens because they develop their most intense leaf colour in cold, frosty weather.

If you have a medium-to-large sized garden, plant tall conifers at the boundary edge. When they are planted within a garden they can take up a huge amount of space and cast considerable shadows behind them.

In a small garden you could create a miniature pinetum using dwarf conifers, including *Pinus mugo* 'Corley's Mat', *Thuja plicata* 'Irish Gold' and *Tsuga canadensis* 'Jeddeloh'. Alternatively, space them around the garden to create a variety of midwinter shapes. Concentrate on extremes, including the round and columnar, especially those like the 5m (15ft) high, 30cm (12in) wide *Juniperus communis* 'Hibernica'.

exciting combinations

Where space permits, try combining and contrasting a number of different shapes. For example, the columnar *Chamaecyparis lawsoniana* 'Green Pillar' goes well with the prostrate junipers *Juniperus procumbens* or *J. squamata* 'Holger'. Others are best as specimen trees in grass or gravel.

In a large garden *Cedrus libani* (cedar of Lebanon) is an automatic first choice for its sensational shape with wide-spreading branches. Equally handsome are its relatives. *Cedrus atlantica* (Atlas cedar) has attractive, fissured bark and a giant height of 40m (130ft). The bark is silver-grey, and the leaves are dark green to greenish-blue. The form 'Aurea' is much slower-growing and has striking bright golden-yellow foliage. *Picea breweriana* (Brewer spruce) and *P. omorika* (Serbian spruce) are also very good choices. The latter has brown bark that cracks into square shapes and leaves tinged with blue.

avenues and dwarfs

Many conifers have special uses. For example, the upright *Taxus baccata* 'Fastigiata' (Irish yew), 5m (15ft) high and 1m (3ft) wide, makes traditional sentry-like shapes to either side of an avenue, framing a vista. You can also try planting dwarf conifers close together so that they grow into each other, assuming a sculptural air. Some form dense mats, particularly *Juniperus horizontalis*, *J. squamata* and *J. procumbens*. Many dwarf conifers are also ideal candidates for rock gardens.

windbreaks

Some conifers make excellent windbreaks. Rapid growers such as x *Cupressocyparis leylandii* grow at 1m (3ft) a year for 20 years, then at 60cm (2ft) a year. Give them space or prune them regularly. Stop them at hedge height, trimming them twice a year, slowing them down and keeping them at about 2m (7ft) high.

above A clever planting scheme showing the range of shapes offered by different, first-rate conifers.

left A collection of large conifers makes a magisterial statement in the depths of winter.

artificial effects

The range of materials that can be used in a garden includes the old and the new. Both can be used in all kinds of ways, and they must either merge with and enhance the existing look, being dictated by the planting scheme and atmosphere, or wittily stand out, catching visitors by surprise. The best gardens have a touch of both, using a wide range, from stone, shells and water to concrete, metal, plastic, stained glass, coloured pebbles, ornamental tiles, paint, wood, artificial lighting and slide projectors. In short, anything goes, but only if it looks good.

statuary

Antique statues are expensive, but it is now possible to buy modern reproductions of such high quality that it is often hard to tell the difference, especially when yogurt has been smeared over them to encourage the growth of lichen.

above The classically proportioned features of an angel adding a nostagic garden touch.

above right Metal discs make an unobtrusive and unusual stepping-stone effect down the length of a gravel path.

Statues can be used as focal points at the end of a vista or wherever there is a quiet part of the garden that needs a dash of grandeur. One grand statue on a plinth in a modest garden will look pompously out of place, but add a couple of smaller, more modest statues, with a face poking out of a border, one behind a pond, or one at the base of a tree, and suddenly you have created the right context for the first statue, and it will look entirely appropriate.

right The perfectly proportioned outline of a statue of a goose waddling across a lawn.

modern materials

Using modern materials in gardens does not mean that they must stand out like eyesores. Rusty metal discs or hub caps can be used to enhance a traditional gravel path, contributing to a rustic look. Replace them with shiny aluminium discs, and the look is lively, upbeat and 21st century. In both cases they inject a sense of movement, especially if the discs are packed close together at the beginning of the path, gradually being spaced further and further apart in the distance to make the path seem longer than it is.

Modern materials can also be used to create a stylish, elegant look. Traditional, high-quality Victorian arbours were incredibly ornate, with intricate wrought-iron patterning, but they can also be bare and minimalist, being used like a picture frame to highlight a topiarized plant. Modern sculptures can be used in witty ways. An elongated, angular face, unlike a rounded classical one, is just the right shape for a grassy, punk-like wig of hair. And the whole effect is softened when other grasses are planted nearby.

above A modern version of an old-fashioned arbour, here used to frame a stylish blue-grey box planter.

a sense of style

If artificial effects begin to dominate the planting, it becomes more of a gallery or playground than a garden. The only time when that does not matter is when you are creating a children's garden.

Although anything goes that gives pleasure, it is usually best to stick to a theme. A path with discs can become a river with stepping stones leading to a monster's lair. Sculptured heads can be given a devilish twist with a coat of paint, giant spiders' webs can be made using lengths of cane, topiarized shrubs may become monsters, and hiding places can be created by close-planting upright shrubs in a semi-circle. If you are artistic, create a mosaic design on a plain wall (perhaps a dull garage) or use oil-based paints to add a *trompe l'oeil* door, apparently opening mysteriously to a secret garden beyond.

left A beautiful, highly inventive combination of a sculptured face with a hollow in the skull for planting a mop of hair-like grass.

pots and tubs

above Evergreen grasses, such as forms of *Festuca*, and bamboos are ideal container plants.

top right This winter-flowering hanging basket contains many evergreen plants, including variegated ivies and *Euphorbia myrsinites*. The blooms of heathers and *Viburnum tinus* add extra interest, but the highlight of the basket is the little *Iris* 'Pauline'.

right The bright yellow flowers of *Eranthis hyemalis* (winter aconite).

When choosing plants for a winter container, see what is available in the garden. There are dozens of small flowering plants at this time of year, and while many are grown under deciduous trees, where they spread freely, many can also be grown in pots to add colour inside the home.

An excellent example is *Eranthis hyemalis* (winter aconite). It has bright yellow flowers offset by highly attractive leaves. You can also grow *Cyclamen coum* or its more tender relative, *C. persicum*. Cyclamen have sweetly-scented pink, red or white flowers through the winter months. Do not keep them in a warm, dry room, however; they need a cool, airy place. This is also the time of year to wander round the garden collecting shapely stems (*Corylus avellana* 'Contorta') and scented flowers (*Hamamelis mollis*) for `display.

window boxes

There are many small plants that can be grown in window boxes and small containers, such as scented hyacinths and hellebores, trailing *Hedera* (ivy), *Ophio-pogon planiscapus* 'Nigrescens', and young phormiums.

Many ivies have leaves that turn an attractive chocolate-brown colour over winter, especially when caught by a frost. They also come in a variety of leaf shapes, from the large to the small and intricate, and many have excellent variegation. The *Ophiopogon* looks like a black-coloured grass, and makes a good contrast with brighter greens. And phormiums, especially *P. tenax* 'Dazzler', have red, orange and pink leaves. Eventually it will get too big for a container and can be planted outside. If it is going from a warm atmosphere to a cold one, make sure that it gradually acclimatizes to its new conditions and provide a deep, dry mulch for winter protection.

above left Hellebores in full flower add plenty of colour just after the winter and into early spring.

above right A stunning combination of young plants for a window box.

left Richly scented, pure white hyacinths look striking in terracotta pots.

WINTER TASKS

A well-planned garden will be packed with colour and interest in the winter months, and working outdoors can be a real pleasure. No matter what the weather, there are always jobs to be done, and tackling them relieves the pressure in spring. Sometimes there is no choice but to become an armchair gardener, however, and this is the time to scan gardening books and plant encyclopedias for ideas to plan minor improvements or to redesign a bed or border or even the whole of your garden, and, of course, to make lists of all those seeds you need to order.

left *Galanthus* 'Atkinsii' early on a frosty winter morning.

above Service your lawn mower and prepare it for storage over the winter.

early winter

The onset of winter inevitably means fewer jobs to do in the garden, but it is a good idea to get outdoors whenever the weather is favourable. There is always tidying-up to be done, and jobs like broken fences to be mended. It makes sense to get work like this finished before the more severe winter weather makes them less appealing. This is an especially good time to take a critical look at how you can improve your soil in time for the next growing season.

Heavy clay soil needs breaking up with horticultural sand and grit and mushroom compost. Fork it in, and smash down thick lumps of soil with the back of a spade, breaking them into pieces. Conversely, poor, thin soil, especially over chalk, will need improving with well-rotted manure. This is demanding work, best done whenever you have time in winter.

plants at their best

* *Chimonanthus praecox*
* *Erica carnea*
* *Erica x darleyensis*
* *Hamamelis mollis*
* *Iris unguicularis* (syn. *I. stylosa*)
* *Ilex*, berries
* *Jasminum nudiflorum*
* *Mahonia x media* 'Lionel Fortescue' and 'Charity'
* *Nerine bowdenii*
* *Gaultheria*, berries
* *Prunus x subhirtella* 'Autumnalis'
* *Pyracantha*, berries
* *Sarcococca*
* *Viburnum x bodnantense*
* *Viburnum farreri*
* *Viburnum tinus*

above Use pegs and string to create a new vegetable bed. Remove weeds and all their roots, and dig in plenty of well-rotted organic matter to improve the soil structure.

above Protect low-growing winter-flowering plants such as *Helleborus niger* from mud and rain damage if you want to cut the blooms for indoors.

the flower garden

* Test your soil
* Keep weeding when shoots appear
* Check bulbs, corms and tubers in store
* Dispose of garden refuse by burning or composting where possible
* Service your mower or have it done professionally
* Plant bare-root and balled trees and shrubs
* Check all bulbs being grown in pots for early flowering
* Protect vulnerable plants that will remain in the garden
* Order seeds
* Take hardwood shrub cuttings
* Take root cuttings
* Plant hedges
* Install a pond heater if you live in a cold area where thick ice is a problem
* Remove leaves that have fallen on rock plants
* Cover alpines that need protection from winter wet with a pane of glass
* Protect flowers of winter plants that might be spoilt by the weather

above If you do not have a cloche, improvise with a piece of polythene (plastic) over wire hoops, or a pane of glass supported on bricks.

the greenhouse and conservatory

❖ Once a week check all plants and pick off any dead or dying leaves before they start to rot
❖ Ventilate on warm days, especially if the greenhouse is well insulated. Poor air circulation can encourage diseases
❖ Except for winter-flowering plants that are still in strong, active growth, gradually give plants less water. Most will then tolerate low temperatures better and diseases should be less of a problem
❖ Put up new shelves and surfaces if required, in readiness for next spring
❖ Check against mice
❖ Buy new pots to replace any that were broken last summer

above Check bulbs and corms in store for any signs of rot. It is worth dusting them with a fungicide suitable for this purpose. Be careful not to inhale any of the dust.

above If you plan to keep your bulbs to grow in the garden, deadhead them as soon as the display is over. This will avoid energy being wasted on seed production.

above Do not plant the bulbs directly into the garden, but acclimatize them gradually in a cold frame or another protected place, such as an unheated greenhouse.

above Plant the bulbs out in a border where they can be left undisturbed.

midwinter

If you made an early start with winter jobs such as digging and tidying beds and borders, midwinter is mainly a time for indoor jobs including ordering seeds and plants, writing labels and designing improvements for the year ahead. These are not unimportant tasks, and by attending to them in good time you are more likely to make the right decisions and have everything ready for late winter and early spring when gardening begins in earnest.

above Sow seeds for summer flowers. Spread them thinly and as evenly as possible.

the flower garden

❖ Keep an area of water open in an iced-over pond if there is a prolonged freeze. If you don't have a pond heater, try standing a pan of boiling water on the ice until it melts through

❖ Knock heavy snow off hedges and conifers if the branches start to bend under the weight. If you leave it, the shape may be spoilt

❖ Insulate the cold frame for extra protection against the coldest weather

❖ Create new paths, making sure that they are not under deciduous trees where leaves will fall, creating a slippery surface

❖ Create new ponds. Aim for a minimum surface area of 12 sq m (130 sq ft). The more it fills with rain over winter the better, because tap water contains chemicals that lead to the growth of algae in hot summer weather

❖ Use lengths of hosepipe to map out new flower beds, and check that you are happy with the shape. Also make sure that the paths between new beds are wide enough for a wheelbarrow and lawnmower

❖ Avoid walking on wet grass on heavy clay because you will create bumps and dips

above Take chrysanthemum cuttings from a clump of roots that has been overwintered in a greenhouse or cold frame. Choose shoots coming directly from the base of the plant.

above Space the chrysanthemum cuttings evenly around the edge of a pot containing a potting mixture that is suitable for cuttings.

above To take root cuttings, lift a well-established plant to provide the cuttings or remove soil from one side of the parent plant to gain access to the roots.

the greenhouse and conservatory

❖ Once a week check all plants and pick off any dead or dying leaves
❖ Continue ventilating, especially on mild days, but even on cold days for at least 30 minutes. This particularly applies where paraffin heaters are being used because they release small quantities of noxious fumes
❖ Water pot plants, but note that being dormant they only need the occasional drink when dry
❖ Paint plant pots for next spring, jazzing them up with smart blue and white stripes, hothouse reds or low-key pale greys
❖ Clean the greenhouse thoroughly to reduce the build-up of pests and diseases.

above Cold frames of any kind benefit from a warm blanket thrown over them on cold nights. A piece of old carpet is an alternative.

plants at their best

❖ *Calluna vulgaris*
❖ *Cupressus sempervirens*
❖ *Erica* spp.
❖ *Euonymus fortunei* 'Variegatus'
❖ *Garrya elliptica*
❖ *Helleborus* spp.
❖ *Juniperus scopulorum* 'Skyrocket'
❖ *Lonicera* x *purpusii*
❖ *Pinus patula*
❖ *Prunus serrula*
❖ *Rubus cockburnianus*
❖ *Salix babylonica* var. *pekinensis* 'Tortuosa'
❖ *Skimmia japonica* 'Rubella'
❖ *Tilia platyphyllus* 'Rubra'

above Cut each root into pieces about 5cm (2in) long. Fill a pot with gritty potting mixture and insert the cuttings the right way up, using a dibber or pencil to make the hole.

above When planting cuttings of thin roots, you can lay them out horizontally, evenly spaced over a tray of compost, and then cover them with a thin layer of gritty potting mix.

above Mulching fruit bushes in winter will give them a good start for the rest of the season.

plants at their best

- ❖ *Crocus tommasinianus*
- ❖ *C. chrysanthus*
- ❖ *Cyclamen coum*
- ❖ *Daphne mezereum*
- ❖ *Eranthis hyemalis*
- ❖ *Erica carnea*
- ❖ *Erica x darleyensis*
- ❖ *Galanthus*
- ❖ *Garrya elliptica*
- ❖ *Helleborus niger*
- ❖ *Helleborus orientalis*
- ❖ *Jasminum nudiflorum*
- ❖ *Iris unguicularis*
- ❖ *Iris reticulata*
- ❖ *Muscari armeniacum*
- ❖ *Narcissus* 'February Gold'
- ❖ *Primula x polyantha*
- ❖ *Prunus cerasifera*
- ❖ *Prunus x subhirtella* 'Autumnalis'

late winter

In favourable areas late winter can be almost spring-like, especially in a mild period, but don't be lulled into sowing and planting outdoors too soon. If the weather turns cold, seeds will not germinate, and seedlings and plants may receive such a check to their growth that they do not do as well as those sown or planted later. Concentrate your efforts on indoor sowing, but make the most of frames and cloches, too, for early crops.

One way of getting plants off to an early start (tomatoes and lettuces, for example) is to sow them in small plastic containers, clearly labelled, in a heated greenhouse. This means that when the spring temperatures do pick up, they can be moved outside, under cloches especially at night when the temperatures can suddenly drop. This is also a good time to check the vegetable garden, forking out the roots of perennial weeds. Also continue breaking up heavy lumps on clay soil. If left, the soil will take much longer to heat up in the spring, and the seeds will find it extremely difficult to get off to a flying start.

above Take time to tidy up a rock garden, removing any weeds that have taken root and adding fresh chippings.

the flower garden

- ❖ Plant climbers
- ❖ Mulch beds and borders, especially after a night of heavy rain
- ❖ Insulate the cold frame for extra protection against the coldest weather
- ❖ Sow sweet peas
- ❖ Pinch out tips of autumn-sown sweet peas
- ❖ Tidy up the rock garden and apply fresh stone chippings where necessary
- ❖ Check labels on shrubs and border plants and renew if necessary
- ❖ Lay a new lawn from turf, provided the ground is not frozen nor waterlogged

above Many summer bedding plants sown earlier will be ready to prick out into trays.

above Sow early crops in a cold frame if it is not packed with overwintering plants.

above When taking dahlia cuttings, remove a tiny piece of the parent tuber with a shoot and it should root quickly without a rooting hormone.

the greenhouse and conservatory

❖ Take chrysanthemum cuttings
❖ Pot up chrysanthemums rooted earlier
❖ Take dahlia cuttings
❖ Sow seeds of bedding plants and pot plants
❖ Prick out seedlings sown earlier
❖ Increase ventilation on warm days
❖ Make sure the glass is clean so that the plants receive plenty of light
❖ Clean all pots and trays in readiness for saving spring seed
❖ Clean all garden tools, scraping off mud, and oil the wood of spades and forks

above If you have a greenhouse, now is the time to sow seeds of frost-tender plants for summer bedding. Medium-sized seeds are easily scattered using a folded piece of stiff paper.

above If you do not have a propagator, enclose pots or trays of cuttings in a plastic bag. Use sticks or twigs to support the bag so that the leaves do not come into contact with the plastic.

above Plant new container-grown climbers as long as the ground is not frozen or waterlogged. Apply a mulch at least 5cm (2in) around the plant after the ground has been soaked thoroughly.

above Later, prick out the bedding seedlings and space them out evenly in the tray.

above A beautiful mix of pure white snowdrops and pink *Cyclamen coum*.

notes

Use these pages to note the plants that have done particularly well, as well as those that have failed so that you can build on your experience to achieve the garden of your dreams.

bulbs

Type ....   Planted ....

Variety ....   Flowered ....

....   Tip for next year ....

Type ....   Planted ....

Variety ....   Flowered ....

....   Tip for next year ....

below A stunning showing of hellebores and *Scilla bithynica*.

perennials

Type ....   Planted ....

Variety ....   Flowered ....

....   Tip for next year ....

Type ....   Planted ....

Variety ....   Flowered ....

....   Tip for next year ....

grasses

Type ....   Planted ....

Variety ....   Flowered ....

....   Tip for next year ....

Type ....   Planted ....

Variety ....   Flowered ....

....   Tip for next year ....

shrubs

Type	Pruned ....
Variety	Flowered ....
....	Tip for next year ....
Type	Pruned ....
Variety	Flowered ....
....	Tip for next year ....

climbers

Type	Pruned ....
Variety	Flowered ....
....	Tip for next year ....
Type	Pruned ....
Variety	Flowered ....
....	Tip for next year ....

trees

Type	Pruned ....
Variety	Flowered ....
....	Tip for next year ....

conifers

Type	Pruned ....
Variety	Flowered ....
....	Tip for next year ....
Type	Pruned ....
Variety	Flowered ....
....	Tip for next year ....

above The brilliantly coloured stems of a *Cornus* gleam in winter sun.

below Bright red holly berries and glossy, green leaves covered in snow are evocative of winter.

index

Page numbers in *italic* refer to the illustrations

above Colourful shrubs under a blanket of snow.

23tr, 31bl © John Glover, 17tc © Howard Rice, 21tc © Neil Holmes, 22bl, 25tl © Jerry Pavia, 25br © Mark Bolton, 25bl © Philippe Bonduel, 29bc © Didier Willery, 30bl © Mayer/Le Scanff, 31br © Rachel White, 45tr © Marie O'Hara, 46, 47br © JS Sira, 47tr © Brigitte Thomas; David Markson 9t and 21br, 23br, 42bl, 43b; Peter McHoy;. We would also like to thank Jonathan Buckley, Michelle Garratt and Peter McHoy (pp56–61) for their photographs for this book.

The publisher would like to thank the following people for allowing us to photograph their gardens. Dartington Hall, Devon (Dartington Hall Trust); RHS Rosemoor, Devon; Great Dixter, East Sussex, Diana Boston, The Manor, Hemingford Grey, Cambridgeshire, Ilford Manor p50tl.

Picture credits

Peter Anderson 1, 2, 3, 4–5, 6–7, 8tr, 9br, 16bl, br, 17tl, tr, 20, 21tl, tr, 22tl, tc, tr, 23tl, 25tr, 26, 27, 28, 29bl, 30bc, 32, 33, 35, 36, 37, 44, 45bl, br, 48, 49, 64; Caroline Arber 16tl, 53tl; Jonathan Buckley 42t, 43tr, 50b Ketley's, East Sussex; 51bl Chelsea Flower Show 1999, 54–55 Glen Chantry, Essex; Garden Picture Library 12br, 22bl,

above Viburnum flowers add colour to a winter garden.

Debbie Brown's

50
Easy Party Cakes

MEREHURST

contents

introduction

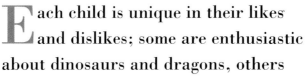

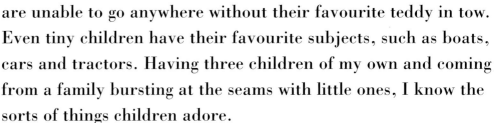

Young boys will enjoy the 'castle guards' cake (above), see page 70. Teenage girls, meanwhile, will appreciate 'shopping frenzy' (above right), see page 42.

Each child is unique in their likes and dislikes; some are enthusiastic about dinosaurs and dragons, others are unable to go anywhere without their favourite teddy in tow. Even tiny children have their favourite subjects, such as boats, cars and tractors. Having three children of my own and coming from a family bursting at the seams with little ones, I know the sorts of things children adore.

In this book, I have put together a collection of cakes that are all exceptionally easy to make and require minimum equipment. Many of the designs are aimed at small children, who love simplified images like the 'toy boat' and 'cute chick'. Other designs will be firm favourites of older children, even teenagers. I have to dedicate 'shopping frenzy' to my daughter, Laura, as she drags me out to the shops all too frequently. The 'camping out' cake made me nostalgic for the time when Lewis, my eldest son, was mad on having garden sleepovers – if only because it was a brilliant excuse for raiding the larder. When my younger son, Shaun, saw the 'castle guards' cake finished, I knew what request I would get for his next birthday!

All children love the idea of 'camping out' in the garden (below), see page 54.

Birthdays are terribly important to children, so I feel that any effort to make their day as special as possible is not wasted. One of the best moments in my cake-making career has to be the sight of a child's face lighting up with wonder and excitement when they see their very own special birthday cake. The little time involved in making it is worth every minute.

equipment

The cakes featured in this book require the minimum of equipment. A **large rolling pin** and **sharp knife** are essential tools. A **sugar shaker** filled with icing/confectioners' sugar is recommended, as are **cocktail sticks**/toothpicks, which are ideal for indenting small details and handy for applying food colouring to the sugarpaste/rolled fondant. Also have to hand a **fine paintbrush**, a **bone modelling tool** and a **small rolling pin**. A smooth, washable kitchen work surface is ideal to work on or, if you prefer, **non-stick work boards** can be obtained in many sizes. Some of the other tools I have used in this book are detailed below. They are all available from cake decorating suppliers and will make useful additions to your workbox.

CAKE SMOOTHER

Used to create a smooth surface on sugarpaste. Different types of smoother are available, but the most useful is a cake smoother with a handle incorporated. Smooth the cake smoother over the sugarpaste in a circular motion to remove bumps and to level out an uneven surface.

CRIMPING TOOL

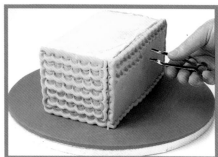

Using a crimping tool is a simple way to add texture and pattern to sugarpaste. The crimping tool pinches up sugarpaste between the pinchers at the end of the tool. Lines are pinched horizontally, letting the serrated teeth scratch vertical lines. First practise on a spare piece of sugarpaste.

PLUNGER CUTTERS

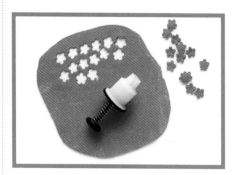

Flowers can be cut quickly using a blossom plunger cutter. Roll out the sugarpaste quite thinly, making sure that it is not sticking to the work surface. Press the cutter down into the sugarpaste and lift out. Rub your finger over the bottom of the cutter to remove excess and ensure a clean shape.

basic recipes

MADEIRA SPONGE CAKE

The secret of successful cake decorating is to use a firm, moist cake that can be cut and shaped without crumbling. Madeira cake is a good choice and can be flavoured for variety. To make a Madeira cake follow the steps below. For the ingredients and bakeware required, see pages 8–9.

1 Preheat the oven to 160°C/325°F/Gas 3, then grease and line the bakeware.

2 Sift the self-raising and the plain/all-purpose flour together in a bowl.

3 Put the soft margarine and caster/superfine sugar in a large mixing bowl, and beat until the mixture is pale and fluffy.

4 Add the eggs to the mixture, one at a time with a spoonful of the flour, beating well after each addition. Add any flavouring required (see panel on right).

5 Using a large spoon, fold the remaining flour into the mixture.

6 Spoon the mixture into the bakeware, then make a dip in the top of the mixture with the back of the spoon.

7 Bake in the centre of the oven until a skewer inserted in the centre comes out clean (see pages 8–9 for cooking times).

8 Leave to cool for 5 minutes, then turn out on to a wire rack and leave to cool completely. When cold, store in an airtight container until ready to use.

Madeira cake flavourings

Vanilla Add 1 teaspoon vanilla essence/extract to every 6-egg mixture.

Lemon Add the grated rind and/or the juice of 1 lemon to every 6-egg mixture.

Chocolate Add 2–3 tablespoons unsweetened cocoa powder mixed with 1 tablespoon milk to every 6-egg mixture.

Almond Add 1 teaspoon almond essence/extract and 2–3 tablespoons ground almonds to every 6-egg mixture.

SUGARPASTE

I recommend using ready-made sugarpaste/rolled fondant, which is high quality and is easily available from cake decorating suppliers (see page 111) and supermarkets. The sugarpaste used in this book is a firm, but pliable sugarpaste that smoothes well and keeps its shape when drying. Try different sugarpastes to find your own preference. Alternatively, use the recipe below for a good home-made sugarpaste.

Makes 625g (1¼lb)
• 1 egg white made up from dried egg albumen
• 2 tablespoons liquid glucose
• 625g (1¼lb/4½ cups) icing/confectioners' sugar
• a little white vegetable fat/shortening if required

1 Put the egg white and liquid glucose into a bowl, using a warm spoon for the liquid glucose.

2 Sift the icing sugar into the bowl, adding a little at a time and stirring until the mixture thickens.

3 Turn out on to a work surface dusted with icing sugar and knead the paste until soft, smooth and pliable. If the paste is a little dry and cracked, fold in a little vegetable fat and knead again.

4 Put immediately into a polythene bag, or double wrap in clingfilm/plastic wrap, and store in an airtight container.

Storing the decorated cake
Store in a cardboard cake box in a warm, dry room. NEVER store in the refrigerator; the atmosphere is damp and the cake will spoil. Decorate the cake within one week of baking.

BUTTERCREAM

As well as making a delicious filling between layers of cake, a thin coat of buttercream spread all over the cake fills any small gaps and provides a smooth surface on which to apply the sugarpaste. Buttercream can also be flavoured (see the panel below for further information).

Makes about 500g (1lb/2 cups)
• 125g (4oz/½ cup) butter, softened, or soft margarine
• 1 tablespoon milk
• 375g (12oz/2½ cups) icing/confectioners' sugar, sifted

1 Put the butter or soft margarine into a mixing bowl.

2 Add the milk and/or any flavouring required (see panel below).

3 Sift the icing sugar into the bowl, a little at a time and beating well after each addition, until all the sugar has been incorporated and the buttercream has a light, creamy texture.

4 Store the buttercream in an airtight container until required.

Buttercream flavourings

Vanilla Add 1 teaspoon vanilla essence/extract.

Lemon Replace the milk with 1 tablespoon fresh lemon juice.

Chocolate Mix the milk and 2 tablespoons unsweetened cocoa powder to a paste and add to the mixture.

Coffee Mix the milk and 1 tablespoon instant coffee powder to a paste and add to the buttercream mixture.

ROYAL ICING

Royal icing is a good sugar glue and it can also be used as a cake covering, see the 'sporty spider' cake on page 19. Ready-made royal icing can be obtained in tubes, and also in powder form to which you have to add a little water (follow the instructions on packet). If you prefer to make your own, use the recipe below.

Makes about 280g (9oz/1 cup)
• 1 egg white made up from dried egg albumen
• 250–280g (8–9oz/1¾ cups) icing/confectioners' sugar, sifted

1 Put the egg white into a bowl. Beat in the icing sugar a little at a time, until the icing is firm and glossy and forms peaks when the spoon is pulled out.

2 Cover the bowl with a damp cloth for a few minutes before use.

SUGAR GLUE
Sugar glue is required to stick pieces of sugarpaste together. Egg white made up from powdered egg albumen is a good glue, as is royal icing (see above).

Alternatively, a glue made from gum arabic is popular, which is available from cake decorating suppliers. Mix 1 teaspoon gum arabic powder with a few drops of water to make a thick paste. Store in an airtight container in the refrigerator.

To stick sugarpaste pieces together successfully, slightly dampen the paste with sugar glue using a fine paintbrush. If you apply too much, the piece may slide out of place. Gently press in position, holding for a few moments. If necessary, small pieces of soft foam sponge can be used to support glued pieces until they are dry.

techniques

COVERING CAKE BOARDS

With sugarpaste

Roll out the sugarpaste/rolled fondant, lift and cover the board. Use a cake smoother to give a completely smooth surface. If the sugarpaste has not stuck to the cake board,

lift the sugarpaste around the edge and moisten using a damp paintbrush. Trim any excess from around the edge, slicing downwards with a sharp knife. You might wish to remove the piece of sugarpaste

from the area of cake board on which the cake will sit. Because the cake is moist, the sugarpaste underneath has a tendency to become slightly sticky. Covered boards are best left to dry for at least 12 hours.

With paper

Use the board as a template by placing it face down on to the back of the paper. Cut around the shape, leaving at least 2.5cm (1in) for an overlap. Moisten the cake board edge using a non-toxic glue stick, then smooth overlap around the back, folding or cutting away excess. To protect the cake from the paper, cut a layer of greaseproof paper/wax baking paper for the base of the cake to act as a barrier.

CARVING CAKE

If the cake is to be cut into shapes, store in an airtight container for at least 6 hours after cooling to allow the texture to settle. Use a sharp, serrated knife when sculpting a shape, trimming a little of the cake at a time to prevent cutting too much. However, if a mistake is made and too much cake is removed, do not worry as it can easily be stuck back on with a dab of buttercream.

TRIMMING CAKE BOARD

For a finishing touch to your cake, attach a length of ribbon around the edge of the cake board, using a non-toxic glue stick to secure the ribbon in place. You will need a slightly thicker width of ribbon if the board is covered with sugarpaste/rolled fondant.

COLOURING SUGARPASTE

Add food colouring to the sugarpaste/rolled fondant, a little at a time, with a cocktail stick/ toothpick. Knead into the sugarpaste, adding more until you have the required shade. Wear plastic gloves as the food colouring can stain your hands. Pre-coloured packs are obtainable from cake decorating suppliers and many supermarkets.

USING SUGARPASTE

Knead thoroughly until warm and pliable before rolling out. Roll out on to a work surface covered with a sprinkling of icing/ confectioners' sugar and keep moving around after each roll. Roll to a thickness of 3–4mm (⅛in), unless otherwise stated.

To lift a piece of rolled-out sugarpaste/ rolled fondant, lay the large rolling pin on the centre and flip over the rolling pin. Lift carefully, position, then roll the sugarpaste in place. Use a sharp, plain-edged knife to cut sugarpaste. To avoid the paste 'pulling', cut cleanly downwards. Keep wiping the blade to remove excess, or a layer of sugarpaste will build up and make cuts untidy.

When the sugarpaste is dry, polish the surface with your hands to remove excess icing sugar and to give a sheen.

cake quantities

cake	page	bakeware	eggs	self-raising flour	plain/all-purpose flour	butter/soft margarine	caster/superfine sugar	baking time
hungry bookworm	62	18cm (7in) square tin/pan	3	190g (6oz/1½ cups)	95g (3oz/¾ cup)	190g (6oz/¾ cup)	190g (6oz/¾ cup)	50 mins
football crazy / treasure map	44 / 69	20cm (8in) round tin/pan	4	250g (8oz/2 cups)	125g (4oz/1 cup)	250g (8oz/1 cup)	250g (8oz/1 cup)	50 mins
snake pit	81	23cm (9in) ring mould	4	250g (8oz/2 cups)	125g (4oz/1 cup)	250g (8oz/1 cup)	250g (8oz/1 cup)	50 mins
farm tractor / little blue train	16 / 60	18cm (7in) square tin/pan	4	250g (8oz/2 cups)	125g (4oz/1 cup)	250g (8oz/1 cup)	250g (8oz/1 cup)	1 hour
make-up bag / wise owl	96 / 30	18cm (7in) round tin/pan	4	250g (8oz/2 cups)	125g (4oz/1 cup)	250g (8oz/1 cup)	250g (8oz/1 cup)	1¼ hours
lovable ladybird	102	2 litre (4 pint/10 cup) ovenproof bowl	4	250g (8oz/2 cups)	125g (4oz/1 cup)	250g (8oz/1 cup)	250g (8oz/1 cup)	1½ hours
goody bag	36	15cm (6in) square tin/pan	4	250g (8oz/2 cups)	125g (4oz/1 cup)	250g (8oz/1 cup)	250g (8oz/1 cup)	1¼ hours
flower power	77	20cm (8in) petal-shaped tin/pan	5	315g (10oz/2½ cups)	155g (5oz/1¼ cups)	315g (10oz/1¼ cups)	315g (10oz/1¼ cups)	1¼ hours
spooky tower	104							
pony stable	66							
jewellery box	100							
camping out	54	20cm (8in) square tin/pan	5	315g (10oz/2½ cups)	155g (5oz/1¼ cups)	315g (10oz/1¼ cups)	315g (10oz/1¼ cups)	1 hour
dressing up	14							
shopping frenzy	42							
toy garage	24							
party bags	90							
mini monsters	82							
candy house	74							
abc book	12	25cm (10in) square tin/pan	5	315g (10oz/2½ cups)	155g (5oz/1¼ cups)	315g (10oz/1¼ cups)	315g (10oz/1¼ cups)	1 hour
pig pen	56							
formula 1 car	78							
castle guards	70	(+ 12 shop-bought mini swiss/jelly rolls)						
giant cup cake	98	22 x 9.5cm (8¾ x 3¾in) brioche tin/pan	5	315g (10oz/2½ cups)	155g (5oz/1¼ cups)	315g (10oz/1¼ cups)	315g (10oz/1¼ cups)	1½ hours
building blocks	48	divide mixture equally between 2 x 15cm (6in) square tins/pans	5	315g (10oz/2½ cups)	155g (5oz/1¼ cups)	315g (10oz/1¼ cups)	315g (10oz/1¼ cups)	50 mins
crowning glory	80	20cm (8in) round cake tin/pan	5	315g (10oz/2½ cups)	155g (5oz/1¼ cups)	315g (10oz/1¼ cups)	315g (10oz/1¼ cups)	1 hour
drummer boy	88	divide mixture equally between 2 x 15cm (6in) round tins/pans	5	315g (10oz/2½ cups)	155g (5oz/1¼ cups)	315g (10oz/1¼ cups)	315g (10oz/1¼ cups)	1 hour
playful kitten	20	divide mixture equally between 2 x 1 litre (2 pint/5 cup) bowls	5	315g (10oz/2½ cups)	155g (5oz/1¼ cups)	315g (10oz/1¼ cups)	315g (10oz/1¼ cups)	1¼ hours
smiling sun	87							
dotty dragon	22							
circus clown	52	3 litre (6 pint/15 cup) ovenproof bowl	5	315g (10oz/2½ cups)	155g (5oz/1¼ cups)	315g (10oz/1¼ cups)	315g (10oz/1¼ cups)	1½ hours

cake	page	bakeware	eggs	self-raising flour	plain/all-purpose flour	butter/soft margarine	caster/superfine sugar	baking time
alien spaceship sporty spider baby in a pram Little Bo Peep dippy dinosaur	92 19 64 38 50	2 litre (4 pint/10 cup) ovenproof bowl	5	315g (10oz/2½ cups)	155g (5oz/1¼ cups)	315g (10oz/1¼ cups)	315g (10oz/1¼ cups)	1¾ hours
friendly frog adorable dolphins cute chick	10 35 106	2 litre (4 pint/10 cup) ovenproof bowl & 0.5 litre (1 pint/2½ cup) ovenproof bowl (½ fill the small bowl, then put the remaining mix into the large bowl)	6	375g (12oz/3 cups)	185g (6oz/1½ cups)	375g (12oz/1½ cups)	375g (12oz/1½ cups)	1½ hours 1 hour
fairy toadstool	26	divide mixture equally between 2 x 1 litre (2 pint/5 cup) ovenproof bowls	6	375g (12oz/3 cups)	185g (6oz/1½ cups)	375g (12oz/1½ cups)	375g (12oz/1½ cups)	1½ hours
Noah's ark	32	20cm (8in) square tin/pan & 1.5 litre (3 pint/7½ cup) oval dish (¼ of mixture in the square tin, put remainder into oval dish)	6	375g (12oz/3 cups)	185g (6oz/1½ cups)	375g (12oz/1½ cups)	375g (12oz/1½ cups)	45 mins 1½ hours
skull & crossbones busy bees	59 46	15cm (6in) & 20cm (8in) round tin (⅓rd of mixture in small tin, put remainder into large tin)	6	375g (12oz/3 cups)	185g (6oz/1½ cups)	375g (12oz/1½ cups)	375g (12oz/1½ cups)	50 min 1 hour
toy boat	72	2 litre (4 pint/10 cup) ovenproof bowl	6	375g (12oz/3 cups)	185g (6oz/1½ cups)	375g (12oz/1½ cups)	375g (12oz/1½ cups)	2 hours
mouse house	40	divide mixture equally between 2 x 2 litre (4 pint/10 cup) ovenproof bowls	7	440g (14oz/3½ cups)	220g (7oz/1¾ cups)	440g (14oz/1¾ cups)	440g (14oz/1¾ cups)	1¼ hours
play wigwam	28	divide mixture between 20cm (8in), 18cm (7in) & 10cm (4in) round tins/pans	7	440g (14oz/3½ cups)	220g (7oz/1¾ cups)	440g (14oz/1¾ cups)	440g (14oz/1¾ cups)	1 hour for each cake
dog & bone	94	1 swiss/jelly roll and 4 fairy/cup cakes			NO BAKING NECESSARY			
dream castle	84	3 swiss/jelly rolls 5 mini swiss/jelly rolls			NO BAKING NECESSARY			

friendly frog

Pop a crown on his head and he is Prince Charming in disguise

MATERIALS
- 1 x 2 litre (4 pint/10 cup) & 1 x 0.5 litre (1 pint/2½ cup) bowl-shaped cakes, see page 9
- 30cm (12in) round cake board
- icing/confectioners' sugar in a sugar shaker
- 1.9kg (3lb 13oz) sugarpaste/ rolled fondant
- green, black & yellow food colouring pastes
- 375g (12oz/1½ cups) buttercream
- sugar glue
- dark green edible dusting powder/ petal dust/blossom tint

EQUIPMENT
- large rolling pin
- sharp knife
- cake smoother
- medium paintbrush

USEFUL TIP
When covering the frog's head and body you will be left with unwanted pleats of green sugarpaste. To get rid of these pleats, either carefully stretch them out and smooth them down, or cut the pleats away and smooth the joins closed. Use the cake smoother to ensure a perfect finish.

1 Colour 375g (12oz) of the sugarpaste a muddy green using green food colouring mixed with a touch of black. Using icing sugar to prevent sticking, roll out and cover the cake board completely, trimming excess from around the edge, then put aside to dry. Trim the crust from each cake and slice the tops flat. Turn each cake upside down. Trim the sides of the small bowl-shaped cake to create a dip for the neck. Cut a layer in the large cake and sandwich with buttercream. Sandwich the cakes together, then spread with buttercream.

2 Colour 1.5kg (3lb) of the sugarpaste green. Using 45g (1½oz), pad the face as in the photograph below. Press with your finger to indent each eye socket. Roll out 1kg (2lb) of green sugarpaste and cover the top of the cake, smoothing the sugarpaste over the frog's head and body. Carefully position the cake on the centre of the cake board. Use a cake smoother to smooth the surface. Use the back of the knife to mark the mouth, indenting each corner and the nostrils with the end of the paintbrush.

3 Roll a ball with 7g (¼oz) of green sugarpaste and cut it in half to make the frog's eyelids. Colour 7g (¼oz) of the sugarpaste yellow and a small amount black. Roll two tiny yellow balls and press flat for the highlights, then roll the remaining yellow into a ball and cut it in half to make the eyes. Roll the black into a ball and press flat, then divide it to make the pupils. Assemble in the eye sockets using sugar glue to secure.

4 To make the frog's arms and hands, split a 155g (5oz) piece of green sugarpaste in half and roll two thick sausages, then round off at each end. Slightly flatten one rounded end of each sausage and make a cut in the centre with a sharp knife. Cut again on either side of the central cut, then smooth the sugarpaste to round off. Press the end of the paintbrush between each to separate and make fingers.

5 Split 220g (7oz) of green sugarpaste into two thick sausages to make the legs. Keep the centre of each sausage slightly thicker than the ends. Bend them in half and stick them together with sugar glue, then stick in place on the cake. Using the remaining green sugarpaste, make two feet in the same style as the hands. Leave the cake to dry, then carefully dust circles over the back of the frog using the dark green dusting powder.

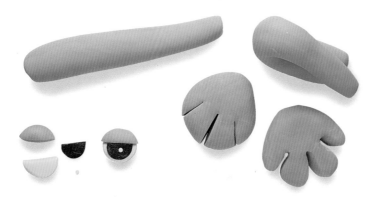

Sugarpaste shapes for the frog's eyes, arms and legs.

Pad the frog's face with pieces of green sugarpaste.

abc book

Parents will try almost anything to encourage little ones to learn their abc

MATERIALS
- 25cm (10in) square cake, see page 8
- 30cm (12in) square cake board
- 200g (6½oz/¾ cup) buttercream
- 1.25kg (2½lb) sugarpaste/ rolled fondant
- icing/confectioners' sugar in a sugar shaker
- green, yellow, brown, orange & black food colouring pastes
- sugar glue
- black food colouring pen

EQUIPMENT
- wrapping paper
- non-toxic glue stick
- scissors
- sharp knife
- large rolling pin
- sheet of greaseproof paper/ wax baking paper
- cocktail stick/toothpick
- bone tool
- 2.5cm (1in) circle cutter

USEFUL TIP
You can use foam pieces to support the modelled fruit in their poses and remove when dry.

1 Cover the cake board with alphabet-patterned wrapping paper (see page 7), securing it with the glue stick. Trim the crust from the cake and slice the top flat with a sharp knife. Trim the centre to create a dip for the book fold and trim the outer edges to slope down. Spread the cake with buttercream to help the sugarpaste stick.

2 Using icing sugar to prevent sticking, roll out white sugarpaste and cover the sides of the cake first, marking the pages with a knife. Cover the top of the cake, trimming excess from around the edge. Cut a piece of greaseproof paper to protect the underside of the cake and position on the centre of the cake board with the cake on top.

3 To create the apple, first colour 125g (4oz) of sugarpaste green. Put aside 7g (¼oz), then roll the remaining green sugarpaste into a ball and indent the top by pressing in with a cocktail stick and rolling it around. Indent eye sockets using the small end of a bone tool and mark the smile with the circle cutter. Make the nose, then model arms with rounded hands and stick in position with sugar glue. Colour 60g (2oz) of sugarpaste black. Using white and black, shape tiny balls of sugarpaste for the eyes.

4 For the banana, first colour 125g (4oz) of sugarpaste pale yellow and 7g (¼oz) brown. Put aside 7g (¼oz) of yellow sugarpaste, then roll the remaining into a sausage tapering at either end and bend it half way. Make the face, nose and arms as for the apple. Shape small, flattened pieces of brown sugarpaste for the top and bottom of the banana.

5 For the carrot, colour 60g (2oz) of sugarpaste orange and roll into a long tapering teardrop shape, marking lines with a knife. Indent the top by pressing in a cocktail stick and rolling it around. Make the face, arms and nose as before. To make the carrot leaf, model a flattened oval shape using green sugarpaste, mark a centre vein with a cocktail stick, then roll the stick along the outer edges to thin and frill. Stick in place with sugar glue.

6 Roll the remaining black sugarpaste into neat, even sausages, and use to shape the letters. Stick the letters on the cake, using sugar glue to secure them in place.

Mark the pages of the book with a knife.

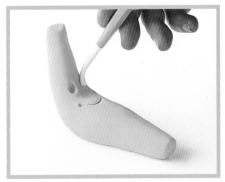
Indent the banana's eyes with a bone tool.

Use a knife to mark lines on the carrot.

dressing up

All girls love dressing up – don't forget the feather boa and lots of pretty hats!

MATERIALS

• 20cm (8in) square cake, see page 8
• 30cm (12in) round cake board
• 1.25kg (2½lb) sugarpaste/rolled fondant
• blue, golden brown, mauve, green, pink & yellow food colouring pastes
• icing/confectioners' sugar in a sugar shaker
• 410g (13oz/1⅔ cups) buttercream
• sugar glue
• black food colouring pen

EQUIPMENT

• large rolling pin
• sharp knife
• ruler
• curved serrated crimping tool
• small circle cutter
• cocktail stick/toothpick
• small, pointed scissors
• blossom plunger cutter, see page 5

USEFUL TIP

If the buttercream has set before you have time to position the sugarpaste sides of the cake, simply add a little more buttercream, or rework the surface.

1 Colour 410g (13oz) of sugarpaste blue. Roll out 375g (12oz) and cover the cake board. Trim the crust from the cake and slice the top flat. Cut the cake in half and sandwich with buttercream. Spread a layer of buttercream over the cake, then position on the board.

2 Colour 500g (1lb) of sugarpaste golden brown. Using a ruler to measure exactly the size required, roll out and cut squares to fit the two ends of the dressing-up box. Crimp around the edge using the serrated crimping tool, then fill in with crimped lines. Carefully position the two ends on the cake. Cover the front and back in the same way.

3 Colour 45g (1½oz) of sugarpaste dark cream using a touch of golden brown food colouring. Roll a ball-shaped nose, then roll the remainder into a ball for the little girl's head. Indent a smile using the circle cutter pressed in at an angle, and dimple each corner using a cocktail stick. Stick the head in position on top of the cake.

4 Colour 125g (4oz) of sugarpaste mauve, 22g (¾oz) green, 60g (2oz) pink, 30g (1oz) cream and the remaining piece of yellow. Roll out some different coloured pieces and position on the cake around the girl's head, encouraging each piece to lie in folds. For the dress, smooth pleats with your fingers on a long, thick piece of mauve sugarpaste. Drape over the front of the basket, then push in the tip of a cocktail stick to mark the pattern.

5 For the hats, shape flattened circles, then top with a dome shape. Roll out and cut a strip for each hat band and stick in place crossing over at the back. Make pink flowers for a hat band for the white hat, using the blossom cutter. To make the bows, shape a bow and indent it in the centre to mark the tie, then indent the pleats using a cocktail stick.

6 To make the tassled scarf, cut a strip of blue sugarpaste, then make little cuts at each end, cutting downwards without pulling or the tassle will break. Create feather boas by rolling sausages of sugarpaste, then snipping up rows of little points using sharp scissors.

7 Roll three thin sausages with cream sugarpaste and plait them together for the girl's hair. Trim with a pink bow. When the cake is dry, draw the girl's eye using the black pen.

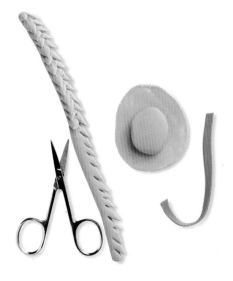

Sugarpaste shapes for a feather boa and hat.

Crimp the sides using a serrated crimping tool.

Position folds of coloured sugarpaste on the cake.

farm tractor

This farmer is ready to roll in from the fields and on to the birthday table

MATERIALS

- 18cm (7in) square cake, see page 8
- 30 x 20cm (12 x 8in) oblong cake board
- 1.75kg (3½lb) sugarpaste/ rolled fondant
- yellow, black, blue, flesh & red food colouring pastes
- icing/confectioners' sugar in a sugar shaker
- 375g (12oz/1½ cups) buttercream
- sugar glue

EQUIPMENT

- large rolling pin
- sharp knife
- ruler
- cocktail stick/toothpick
- 2.5cm (1in) & 3cm (1¼in) circle cutters
- templates, see page 109

USEFUL TIP

Instead of filling the farmer's trailer with yellow sugarpaste straw, you could pile on a few mini chocolate rolls or chocolate sticks to look like logs.

1 Colour 560g (1lb 2oz) of sugarpaste pale yellow. Using icing sugar to prevent sticking, roll out 440g (14oz) and cover the cake board. Press the edge of a ruler over the surface to indent and create a straw effect, then trim excess from around the edge.

2 Trim the crust from the cake and slice the top flat. Cut the cake exactly in half and put one half on top of the other. Cut the top layer in half and take one of the top pieces away. Trim a slope in the back of the piece left on the base. Cut the other piece of cake into an oblong shape for the trailer. Trim at an inward angle around the base of the tractor.

3 Sandwich the layers together using buttercream, then spread a thin layer of buttercream over the surface of each cake. Position the tractor on the cake board. Colour 250g (8oz) of sugarpaste black. Thinly roll out and cut a 2.5cm (1in) deep strip of black to fit around the base of the tractor. Carefully roll up, position the end against the base of the tractor, then wrap around the base, smoothing the join closed.

4 Colour 500g (1lb) of sugarpaste blue. Roll out 345g (11oz) and cover the top of the tractor. Smooth around the shape, then cut away around the base leaving the black strip showing. Roll out the remaining blue sugarpaste and cut pieces to cover all sides of the trailer, then position on the cake board. Roll out the remaining yellow sugarpaste and cut a square the same size as the trailer. Mark with a ruler to create a straw effect as before, stretching out the edges, then position on top of the trailer.

5 To make the farmer, first colour 315g (10oz) of sugarpaste grey and 60g (2oz) flesh. Model a fat teardrop for his body using 90g (3oz) of grey and stick to the tractor with sugar glue. Split a 30g (1oz) piece in half and roll two sausage-shaped arms. Bend each arm half way by pinching in at the elbow, then stick on the farmer's body. Roll 45g (1½oz) of flesh-coloured sugarpaste into a ball for the head, then with the remaining flesh model two ball-shaped hands, an oval nose and two oval ears. Press in the centre of each ear to flatten and stick in place. With 7g (¼oz) of grey sugarpaste, model two teardrop shapes for his moustache, then shape little pieces and stick over his head for the hair.

continued overleaf!

Sugarpaste shapes for the farmer.

Halve the top piece of cake to form the trailer.

Unravel the black strip around the base.

6 Roll 7g (¼oz) of black sugarpaste into a sausage and loop around to make the steering wheel. With the remaining black, roll two tiny eyes, shape a circle measuring 5cm (2in) for the hat rim, then roll a ball and pinch either side for the top of the hat. Indent the hat at the top by pressing in with a cocktail stick. With some of the blue sugarpaste trimmings, roll out and cut the hat band.

7 Colour the remaining sugarpaste red. Using 22g (¾oz), roll a sausage and stick it around the base of the farmer for the tractor seat. With 7g (¼oz), roll a sausage for the funnel, cut both ends straight, then put aside to set for 10 minutes before sticking in place. To make the large tractor wheels, roll two balls from 125g (4oz) of grey sugarpaste. Flatten each ball, then mark the edges with the end of a ruler. Indent the centres of the wheels using the circle cutters, then put aside to set for 10 minutes.

8 With some of the remaining grey sugarpaste, make two small tractor wheels, pressing in the centre of each to indent, and the four trailer wheels. Then, using the templates (see page 109), cut out the grilles. Thinly roll out the grey sugarpaste trimmings and cut to size. Mark lines on the grilles with a ruler. With the remaining red sugarpaste, model flattened balls for the centres of the wheels and the top of the funnel.

Cut pieces of blue sugarpaste to fit each side.

Mark the large wheels with the edge of a ruler.

Model a cute mouse with any remaining grey sugarpaste.

sporty spider

This cheeky spider is sure to pip other contenders to the birthday party table

MATERIALS

- 2 litre (4 pint/10 cup) bowl-shaped cake, see page 9
- 35cm (14in) round cake board
- 1kg (2lb) sugarpaste/rolled fondant
- green, yellow, black, blue & red food colouring pastes
- icing/confectioners' sugar in a sugar shaker
- sugar glue
- 185g (6oz/¾ cup) buttercream
- 140g (4½oz/½ cup) royal icing
- lengths of liquorice/licorice

EQUIPMENT

- large rolling pin
- sharp knife

1 Colour 500g (1lb) of sugarpaste green and 75g (2½oz) yellow. Roll out the green sugarpaste and cover the cake board, trimming excess from around the edge. Thinly roll out the yellow sugarpaste and cut two strips. Stick the strips on to the cake board with sugar glue, then put the board aside to dry. Trim the crust from the cake, keeping the rounded top where the cake has risen.

2 Turn the cake upside down and spread a layer of buttercream over the surface to help the sugarpaste stick. Colour 315g (10oz) of sugarpaste black, thinly roll out and cover the cake completely, smoothing around the shape and tucking the excess underneath. Press a length of liquorice into the surface to indent the spider's smile.

3 Colour the royal icing black. Spread the royal icing over the surface of the cake, covering a little at a time, and stipple by patting with the flat of a knife. Spread a little more royal icing on the top of the cake to create higher peaks.

4 Bend lengths of liquorice and push them into the cake to create the spider's legs. Stipple some more black royal icing around the top of the legs to hold them in place. Model white sugarpaste oval shapes for the running shoes and stick the ends of the liquorice into each shoe using sugar glue. Flatten two large white oval shapes for the eyes. Model two flattened circles for the pupils using the black trimmings. Colour the remaining sugarpaste red and blue. Thinly roll out and cut tiny strips for the running shoes, sticking in place with sugar glue.

Stipple the royal icing with a knife.

playful kitten

A sweet kitten playing with a ball of wool makes an unusual but simple cake

MATERIALS
- 2 x 1 litre (2 pint/5 cup) bowl-shaped cakes, see page 8
- 25cm (10in) round cake board
- 1.75kg (3½lb) sugarpaste/ rolled fondant
- blue, pink & black food colouring pastes
- icing/confectioners' sugar in a sugar shaker
- 280g (9oz/1 generous cup) buttercream
- sugar glue

EQUIPMENT
- large rolling pin
- sharp knife
- small circle cutter

USEFUL TIP
To create a smooth, crack-free sausage shape, roll a small piece of paste into a ball, then gently roll over the work surface, stretching along the length. Don't press down too hard or you will flatten the sugarpaste. Use icing sugar to prevent sticking.

1 Colour 315g (10oz) of sugarpaste blue. Using icing sugar, roll out and cover the cake board completely. For a fabric effect, press the rolling pin on to the cake board surface to form indents, then trim excess sugarpaste from around the edge. Put aside to dry.

2 Trim the crust from each cake and slice the tops flat. Sandwich together with buttercream, then spread a thin layer over the surface to help the sugarpaste stick. Colour 1.25kg (2½lb) of sugarpaste pale pink. Using 500g (1lb), thinly roll out and cover the cake completely. Do not worry if the covering is untidy as this will be hidden later.

3 To make the strands of wool, roll long, thin sausages of sugarpaste and stick over the cake with sugar glue. Apply six or seven strands right across the top of the cake, from the bottom all the way round to the base at the other side. Cover the two remaining sides with diagonal strands which will leave a small triangular shape uncovered at the base. Cover this with vertical strands. Roll a few extra strands and stick them randomly over the cake.

4 Colour 155g (5oz) of sugarpaste black. Using 60g (2oz), roll a teardrop shape for the kitten's body. With 45g (1½oz), roll an oval shape for the head. Roll a thick sausage using 30g (1oz) and cut four short lengths for the legs. With the remaining black, make two triangular-shaped ears, two tiny flattened balls for the pupils and then roll a little pointed tail. Cut two small triangular shapes from the remaining pink sugarpaste to fill in each ear; also model a flattened ball for a collar and shape an oval nose.

5 With a little white sugarpaste, flatten a tiny ball for a muzzle and stick it on to the oval-shaped head. Using a knife, mark a line on the muzzle with a knife, then indent a smile using the circle cutter pressed in at an angle. Just above the muzzle, stick on two small flattened balls of white with two slightly smaller flattened balls of blue at the base, then finally secure the pupils made earlier. Stick the kitten's nose in place.

6 Assemble the kitten on top of the cake. Roll balls of white sugarpaste for the paws and stick in place with sugar glue. To finish, roll a final strand of wool using the last of the pink sugarpaste and stick in position draped around the kitten, falling on to the cake board.

Sugarpaste shapes for the kitten.

Cover with a thin layer of pink sugarpaste.

Stick strands of wool to the cake with sugar glue.

dotty dragon

A dotty dragon with a big round tummy – full of cake I suppose!

MATERIALS

- 2 x 1 litre (2 pint/5 cup) bowl-shaped cakes, see page 8
- 25cm (10 in) round cake board
- 2kg (4lb) sugarpaste/ rolled fondant
- mauve, green, yellow & black food colouring pastes
- icing/confectioners' sugar in a sugar shaker
- 280g (9oz/1 generous cup) buttercream
- sugar glue

EQUIPMENT

- large rolling pin
- sharp knife
- cake smoother
- food-safe plastic dowelling rod
- templates, see page 110
- fine paintbrush

USEFUL TIP

You could stick sugar-coated chocolate buttons, or similar sweets on his back, instead of making sugarpaste dots.

1 Colour 315g (10oz) of sugarpaste mauve. Roll out and cover the cake board, trimming excess from around the edge. Trim the crust from each cake and slice the tops flat. Sandwich the cakes together using buttercream, then spread a layer over the surface.

2 Colour 1.6kg (3lb 3½oz) of sugarpaste green. Using 75g (2½oz), pad out the tail area, tapering the end to a point. Roll 45g (1½oz) into a ball and use to pad the neck area. Roll out 1kg (2lb) of green sugarpaste and cover the cake and tail completely, smoothing around the shape. Cut away any pleats and smooth the joins closed.

3 Position the cake on the cake board and smooth the surface with a cake smoother. To help support the head, push a dowelling rod down through the neck, leaving 5cm (2in) protruding from the top. Roll 280g (9oz) of green sugarpaste into a ball for the head, then pinch around the top to narrow and give height. Push the head down on to the dowelling rod, securing it in place with a little sugar glue at the base.

4 Cut a wide mouth, pulling down the bottom lip slightly. Push the end of the fine paintbrush into the mouth corners to dimple, then push in for the nostrils at the front. Using 7g (¼oz) of green sugarpaste, shape two pointed ears and stick in place. Roll two white balls for the eyes, then colour a tiny amount of sugarpaste black and make the pupils.

5 Colour the remaining sugarpaste yellow. Using the template (see page 110), thinly roll out and cut the dragon's tummy patch. Stick in place, then mark lines using the back of a knife. Split 75g (2½oz) of green sugarpaste in half. Create two teardrop shapes for the feet and make two cuts to separate the toes. To make the arms, split 75g (2½oz) of green sugarpaste in half. Roll a sausage with a rounded end and make two cuts to separate the fingers, smoothing to remove ridges. Stick in position, then make the other arm as before.

6 With 7g (¼oz) of green sugarpaste, shape a triangle for the pointed tail. Roll out the remaining green and cut two wings using the template (see page 110). Roll the side of the paintbrush into the surface to indent, then stick in place with sugar glue. To finish, stick small, flattened balls over the dragon's back using the trimmings of mauve sugarpaste.

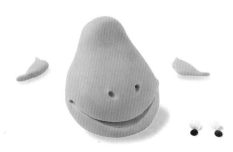

Sugarpaste shapes for the dragon's head.

Indent the dragon's wings with a paintbrush.

Use sugarpaste to pad the neck and tail.

toy garage

Be prepared for a traffic jam at the party table when you serve this cake

MATERIALS
- 20cm (8in) square cake, see page 8
- 30cm (12in) square cake board
- 2kg (4lb) sugarpaste/ rolled fondant
- black, red, green, blue, yellow & cream food colouring pastes
- icing/confectioners' sugar in a sugar shaker
- 410g (13oz/1⅓ cups) buttercream
- sugar glue

EQUIPMENT
- large rolling pin
- sharp knife
- cake smoother
- miniature circle cutter

Model each car from a ball of sugarpaste.

1 Colour 750g (1½lb) of sugarpaste grey using a touch of black food colouring paste. Roll out 440g (14oz) and cover the cake board, trimming excess from around edge, then put aside to dry. Trim the crust from the cake and slice the top flat. Cut in half and put one half on top of the other. Trim one end to curve around, then sandwich the layers together with buttercream. Spread a layer of buttercream over the surface of the cake.

2 Roll out 75g (2½oz) of white sugarpaste and cut a piece to fit the square end of the cake, then press into position. Roll out 375g (12oz) of white and cut an oblong to fit around the cake sides. Roll up, position against the cake, then unroll around the cake.

3 Roll out 200g (6½oz) of grey. Carefully place the top of the cake down on to it and cut around, then turn the cake over and position on the board. Colour 280g (9oz) red. Roll out 100g (3½oz) and cut a strip to fit around the top of the cake, sticking with sugar glue.

4 Using the remaining grey, roll out and cut two strips for the road ramps, sticking securely at the top and bottom with sugar glue. To make the petrol pumps, roll a sausage with 75g (2½oz) of white sugarpaste and press a little flat, then cut in half. Colour 60g (2oz) of sugarpaste black. Make the petrol pump hoses using a little red and black.

5 Colour 15g (½oz) of sugarpaste cream, 30g (1oz) yellow and 200g (6½oz) blue. To make the little people, model a ball of paste, pressing a little flat. Cut the bottom straight to make the body. Roll balls of cream sugarpaste for each head, marking a smile using the circle cutter pressed in at an angle. Roll tiny noses and eyes, sticking in place with sugar glue. For the caps, model flattened circles, then pinch up one side for a peak. Make the ramps and road markings with black, white and yellow sugarpaste.

6 Colour the remaining sugarpaste green. To make the cars and truck, model a ball of sugarpaste and press gently on the top to flatten slightly. With the flat of a knife, press into the sugarpaste to mark the front window, then press down to flatten the bonnet. Shape the back of the car in the same way. Cut straight edges all around each car. Make the truck, but keep the back square. Shape tyres from black sugarpaste, indenting each with your finger.

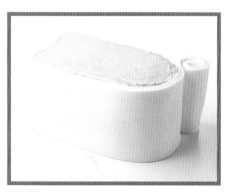

Unroll the white sugarpaste around the cake.

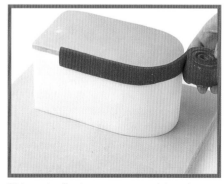

Stick a strip of red sugarpaste around the cake.

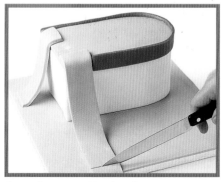

Create the ramps with strips of grey sugarpaste.

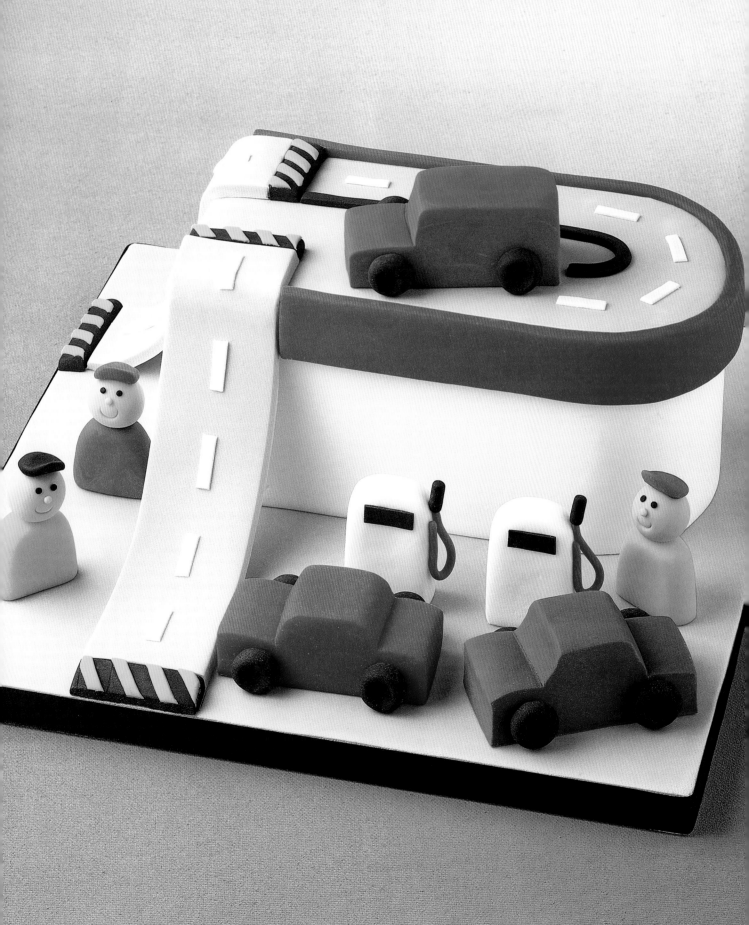

fairy toadstool

All little girls will love this magical house with sparkling fairies all around

MATERIALS

- 2 x 1 litre (2 pint/5 cup) bowl-shaped cakes, see page 9
- 25cm (10in) petal-shaped cake board
- 1.25kg (2½lb) sugarpaste/rolled fondant
- green, pink, yellow, mauve, blue, peach & cream food colouring pastes
- icing/confectioners' sugar in a sugar shaker
- 375g (12oz/1½ cups) buttercream
- sugar glue
- tiny star-shaped sweets/candies
- hundreds and thousands/sprinkles
- edible sparkle powder/ petal dust/blossom tint

EQUIPMENT

- large rolling pin
- sharp knife
- templates, see page 109
- miniature, small, medium & large circle cutters
- cocktail stick/toothpick
- No. 2 plain piping tube/tip
- silver ribbon
- medium paintbrush

1 Colour 315g (10oz) of sugarpaste green. Roll out and cover the cake board, trimming around the edge before putting aside to dry. Trim the crust from each cake and slice the top of one of the cakes flat. Turn this cake over to form the base of the toadstool.

2 Hollow out the centre of the second cake to make the roof. Keep a rounded edge and level off where the cake has risen before cutting down a further 2.5cm (1in). Trim the sides so the roof edge is slightly uneven. Turn the cake upside down and trim a ridge around the top to create a sloping roof. Spread a layer of buttercream over both cakes.

3 Cover the base of the toadstool with 345g (11oz) of white sugarpaste, trimming the excess from around the edge. Place on the board. Colour 470g (15oz) of sugarpaste pink. Roll a 60g (2oz) ball and use to pad the roof. Roll out 375g (12oz) and cover the roof cake, tucking the sugarpaste underneath. Using sugar glue, stick the roof on the base.

4 Roll out the remaining pink sugarpaste and cut out the door and windows using the templates (see page 109) and the miniature circle cutter. Mark a woodgrain effect on the door with a knife. Cut wedges of white sugarpaste for the frames. To make the petal shutters, press a tiny ball of sugarpaste flat and pinch around the edge to thin and frill. Stick in place with sugar glue. Thinly roll out and cut white sugarpaste circles for the roof.

5 To make the fairies, split 7g (¼oz) of sugarpaste into five pieces, one slightly larger. Colour the largest piece yellow and the others dark pink, mauve, blue and peach. Colour 7g (¼oz) cream. Create a long, tapering teardrop shape for each body. For the arms, roll a thin sausage tapering at the ends with cream sugarpaste and stick on the body. Roll tiny cream heads and indent the smiles by pressing in the piping tube at an angle. Mark the eyes with a cocktail stick. For the hair, roll a sausage of yellow tapering in at either end and press flat, then curl the ends. Tie five silver bows and stick to each fairy with sugar glue.

6 Moisten the cake board with sugar glue, then sprinkle on the stars to make a path. Stick stars to the front of each fairy and use one for a door handle. Sprinkle hundreds and thousands around the cake. Dust with sparkle powder using a medium paintbrush.

Sugarpaste shapes for the fairies' heads and bodies.

Shape the two cakes to form the toadstool.

Stick the doors and windows on to the cake.

play wigwam

Cowboy and Indian fans will love this cake made in the shape of a wigwam

MATERIALS

- 20cm (8in), 18cm (7in) & 10cm (4in) round cakes, see page 9
- 25cm (10in) round cake board
- 1.35kg (2¾lb) sugarpaste/rolled fondant
- green, black, yellow, red, blue, cream & brown food colouring pastes
- icing/confectioners' sugar in a sugar shaker
- 440g (14oz/1¾ cups) buttercream
- sugar glue
- chocolate stick

EQUIPMENT

- large rolling pin
- sharp knife
- 4cm (1½in), 2.5cm (1in) & 1cm (½in) square cutters
- miniature circle cutter
- cocktail stick/toothpick

USEFUL TIP

Press the circle cutter in at an angle when marking the little boy's smile. Create dimples by pushing the tip of a cocktail stick into each corner of the smile and lifting slightly.

1 Colour 315g (10oz) of sugarpaste green. Roll out and cover the cake board, trimming excess from around the edge, then put aside to dry. With trimmings, shape two cactus and put aside. Trim the crust from each cake and slice the tops flat. Stack the cakes together, graduating in size. Trim from the top, cutting downwards, removing the top edge of each cake to create the sloping sides of the wigwam. Sandwich the layers together with buttercream, then spread a layer over the surface of the cake to help the sugarpaste stick.

2 Colour 30g (1oz) of sugarpaste black. Reserve a tiny amount for the boy's eyes, then thinly roll out the remainder and cover the front of the cake for the opening. Place the cake on the board. Colour 875g (1¾lb) of sugarpaste yellow. Using a small piece, cover the top of the cake. Roll out the remaining yellow and cut an oblong measuring 50 × 22cm (20 × 8½in). Carefully roll up, place a straight edge against the front of the cake by the black strip, then unroll around the cake, keeping the top smooth and neat against the cake. This will create excess at the bottom, so trim away until level with the opposite side. Trim at the join, smoothing open at the centre. Pinch around the top of the wigwam, creating a lip.

3 Colour 45g (1½oz) red and 22g (¾oz) blue. Thinly roll out red and cut squares from squares using the cutters. Cut in half to make 'v' shapes, and stick around the wigwam creating a zigzag pattern. Thinly roll out blue and cut small squares, sticking in place following the zigzag pattern. Mark two line patterns using a knife. Using sugar glue, stick the cactus in place. Break the chocolate stick into three pieces and push gently into the top of the wigwam.

4 Colour 35g (1¼oz) of sugarpaste cream and 7g (¼oz) brown. For the boy, model two teardrop shapes for hands, an oval nose and two ears, pressing in the centre of each to indent, then roll the remaining piece into an oval-shaped head. Stick the nose in place. Mark his smile by pressing in with the circle cutter. Stick in place with sugar glue.

5 Thinly roll out blue trimmings and cut a strip for the head band and stick around his forehead. Model three teardrop shapes for the feathers using trimmings and press flat. Indent down the centre of each and gently cut lines either side. Stick on two oval-shaped eyes. Stick different sized pieces of brown sugarpaste over the boy's head for his hair.

Cut decorative shapes with the square cutters.

Stack the layers of cake together with buttercream.

Unroll the yellow sugarpaste around the cake.

wise owl

Certainly a different way of encouraging children to do their sums

1 Colour 375g (12oz) of sugarpaste black. Using icing sugar to prevent sticking, roll out and cover the cake board completely, trimming excess from around the edge and put aside to dry. Cover the square cake card in the same way, using the black trimmings. Trim the crust from the cake and slice the top flat. Cut a 2.5cm (1in) wedge from the cake to create the base of the owl. Cut two more wedges from either side, slanting up to the top to shape the owl. Spread the cake with buttercream to help the sugarpaste stick.

2 Knead orange and yellow food colourings into 750g (1½lb) of sugarpaste until it is slightly streaky. Thinly roll out 100g (3½oz) of this orange-yellow sugarpaste and place the back of the cake down on to it. Cut around the shape of the cake. Cover the front of the cake in the same way and then position the cake on the board. Thinly roll out another 100g (3½oz) of orange-yellow and cut a strip to cover the top of the cake and down the sides. Don't worry if the cake covering is untidy as this will be covered later.

3 Roll out 75g (2½oz) of white sugarpaste and cut the tummy patch using the template (see page 110). Roll out 30g (1oz) of white and cut a circle using the large cutter. Trim a 'v' from the top and bottom to make the owl's face. Using 315g (10oz) of the orange-yellow sugarpaste, thinly roll out and cut petal shapes for the owl's feathers, sticking them around the base first, then build up around the cake and cover the first layer of sugarpaste.

4 With the remaining orange-yellow sugarpaste, model two pointed ears, indenting in the centre of each with your finger. Create six long teardrop shapes. Stick three teardrop shapes on to either side of the cake for each wing. Colour 100g (3½oz) of sugarpaste yellow. Using 45g (1½oz), shape three tapering teardrop shapes into a foot, sticking in place graduating in size. Make the other foot in the same way. With the remaining yellow, shape a pointed beak with two teardrop shapes, the top one thicker than the other.

5 With sugar glue, stick the cake card on top of the owl's head. With black, model small flattened ovals for the pupils, then roll out and cut the glasses using the circle cutters and cut strips for the hat tassle. Using white, model flattened oval shapes for eyes and a tiny highlight for each eye. Thinly roll out and cut numbers to decorate the cake board.

Shape the cake with a sharp knife.

Use white sugarpaste for the owl's tummy and face.

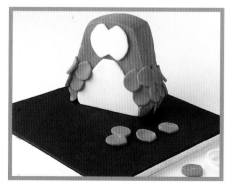
Cut petal shapes to create the owl's feathers.

Noah's ark

If time is short, use small animal toys instead of these modelled animals

MATERIALS
- 1 x 1.5 litre (3 pint/7½ cup) oval cake & 1 x 20cm (8in) square cake, see page 9
- 20cm (8in) round cake board
- 440g (14oz/1¾ cups) buttercream
- 2kg (4lb) sugarpaste/ rolled fondant
- black, brown, yellow, blue, pink & golden-brown food colouring pastes
- icing/confectioners' sugar in a sugar shaker
- sugar glue

EQUIPMENT
- sharp knife
- large rolling pin
- cocktail sticks/toothpicks
- fine paintbrush
- small circle cutter
- small pieces of foam sponge

USEFUL TIP
Instead of colouring the sugarpaste brown, you could use chocolate sugarpaste as a delicious alternative.

1 Cut the crust from each cake and slice the tops flat. Cut the square cake into four equal sized squares and stack one on top of the other. Make sure they sit evenly, then trim either side to create the sloping roof, cutting down two layers only. Sandwich the layers together with buttercream. Cut a layer in the oval-shaped cake and sandwich back together with buttercream, then spread a thin layer of buttercream over both cakes.

2 Colour 280g (9oz) of sugarpaste black. Using icing sugar to prevent sticking, roll out 220g (7oz) of black and place the top of the oval-shaped cake down on to it. Cut around the shape, then pick the cake up and position on the centre of the cake board.

3 Colour 875g (1¾lb) of sugarpaste brown. Roll out and cut strips about 2cm (¾in) wide. Cut these strips into different lengths and texture the surface of each, using a knife to give a wood effect. Cover the bottom cake with these strips, working from the base upwards. Mark little holes at the end of each plank using the end of a cocktail stick. Cover the cabin in the same way, leaving the roof uncovered. Cut four thin strips and secure vertically on each side of the ark with sugar glue.

4 Cut two holes on either side of the cabin and remove the sugarpaste. Thinly roll out some black sugarpaste and cut two circles to fill these gaps. Roll a thin sausage of black sugarpaste and twist into a loop for the door on the side of the ark.

5 Colour 155g (5oz) of sugarpaste pale yellow. To make the roof, roll out 125g (4oz) of yellow and cut two pieces to fit either side of the roof. Keeping the cut pieces of yellow sugarpaste flat on the work surface, mark a straw effect with a sharp knife, taking care not to cut too deeply into the sugarpaste. Pull the knife downwards to stretch and fray the bottom edge, then position the pieces on the top of the cake.

6 Colour 185g (6oz) of sugarpaste blue. Roll out the blue sugarpaste and press it on to the cake board around the ark. Use your fingertips to create an uneven water effect, then trim any excess from around the edge of the cake board.

continued overleaf/

Model the giraffe's head from yellow sugarpaste.

Sugarpaste shapes for the elephant's head and ears.

Stack the cut cakes together to form the ark.

Cover the sides with strips of brown sugarpaste.

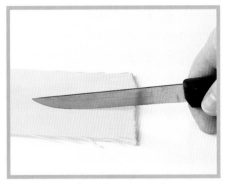

Create a straw effect using a sharp knife.

7 To make the animals, first colour 170g (5½oz) of sugarpaste yellow, 125g (4oz) grey, 30g (1oz) pink, 15g (½oz) pale brown and 15g (½oz) golden brown. Use these pieces of coloured sugarpaste and the remaining pieces of pale yellow, black and white sugarpaste.

8 Each animal head is shaped from a ball of coloured sugarpaste. When a long muzzle is needed, pinch at one side of the ball, twisting the sugarpaste to form a rounded end. To create the giraffe, also pinch underneath the ball of sugarpaste to make the neck. For the elephant, twist the sugarpaste until long for the trunk and taper it in at the end.

9 Indent the nostrils with the end of a paintbrush, or use a cocktail stick. Mark smiles using the circle cutter pressed in at an angle. The zebra and tiger stripes are created with tiny uneven sausages of black sugarpaste pressed flat. The patches on the giraffe and snake are tiny different sized balls of sugarpaste, also pressed flat.

10 When all the animals have been made, place them on the ark in pairs. Cut two holes in the top of the roof for the giraffes' heads, and secure them in position with sugar glue. You may need to use small pieces of foam sponge for support whilst drying.

Decorate the cake with a variety of different animals. Remember that all the animals should be in pairs!

adorable dolphins

Two cute dolphins make the perfect cake for any child who loves the sea

MATERIALS

• 1 x 2 litre (4 pint/10 cup) &
1 x 0.5 litre (1 pint/2½ cup)
bowl-shaped cakes, see page 9
• 35cm (14in) round cake board
• 1.75kg (3½lb) sugarpaste/rolled fondant
• mauve, dark green, dark blue,
pink & black food colouring pastes
• icing/confectioners' sugar
in a sugar shaker
• 375g (12oz/1½ cups) buttercream
• sugar glue

EQUIPMENT

• large rolling pin
• sharp knife
• bone tool

Pad the cakes with grey sugarpaste.

1 Split 500g (1lb) of sugarpaste into four and colour mauve, dark green, dark blue and pink. Put aside 15g (½oz) of dark green, then knead the remaining colours into one another until streaky. Roll out and cover the cake board. Press over the surface with your fingers to indent. Trim excess from around the edge and put aside to dry.

2 Trim the crust from each cake, keeping the tops rounded where they have risen. Spread the surface with buttercream to help the sugarpaste stick. Colour the remaining sugarpaste grey using a little of each of the black and mauve food colouring pastes.

3 Using 155g (5oz) of the grey sugarpaste, model a teardrop shape and place at the base of the large bowl cake to form the padding for the tail end. Roll tapering sausages using 60g (2oz) and press on to the opposite side of the large cake to pad the dolphin's face. Roll out the remaining grey sugarpaste and cover the cake completely, smoothing around the shape, then trim the excess sugarpaste from around the edge.

4 With your finger, smooth into the mouth to indent a smile, then position the dolphin on the cake board. Gently push the large end of a bone tool into the sugarpaste to indent eye sockets. Cover the other bowl cake in the same way, using 75g (2½oz) of sugarpaste to pad the tail end and 30g (1oz) to pad the face.

5 Shape all the fins using the remaining grey sugarpaste and stick in place with sugar glue. Colour a pea-sized amount of sugarpaste trimmings black and model four tiny eyes. For the seaweed, roll different sized sausages of dark green sugarpaste, then pinch along the length to indent. Leave to set for a few moments before sticking them in position around the dolphins with sugar glue.

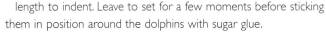
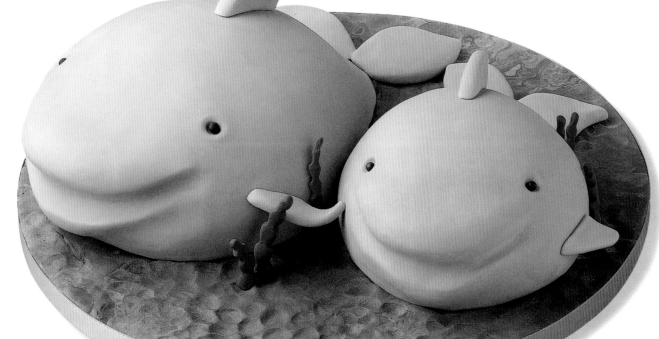

goody bag

A dream cake – so many sweets spilling out that there is no room for the candles!

MATERIALS
- 15cm (6in) square cake, see page 8
- 25cm (10in) round cake board
- 1kg (2lb) sugarpaste/ rolled fondant
- pink, orange & yellow food colouring pastes
- icing/confectioners' sugar in a sugar shaker
- 345g (11oz/1⅓ cups) buttercream
- assorted sweets/candies
- sugar glue

EQUIPMENT
- large rolling pin
- sharp knife

USEFUL TIP
As an alternative, fill the bag with sugar-coated chocolates, and use the chocolates to decorate the bag instead of flattened balls of sugarpaste.

1 Colour 750g (1½lb) of sugarpaste pink and 185g (6oz) orange. Using icing sugar to prevent sticking, roll out all the orange sugarpaste and 185g (6oz) of the pink sugarpaste and cut 2.5cm (1in) wide strips. Following the photograph below, stick alternate coloured strips over the cake board, trimming excess sugarpaste from around the edge. Put the covered board aside to dry.

2 Trim the crust from the cake with a sharp knife and slice the top flat. Cut the cake in half and put one half on top of the other. Trim the cake at each corner to round off. Sandwich the two cakes together with buttercream, then spread a thin layer of buttercream over the surface of the cake to help the sugarpaste stick.

3 Using the remaining pink sugarpaste, roll out and cut a strip measuring 42 × 15cm (17 × 6in). Carefully roll up this pink sugarpaste strip, position it against the side of the cake, then unroll it around the cake, securing the join with sugar glue.

4 Pinch around the top edge of the sugarpaste to thin and to frill the edges of the bag. Dampen your fingers with water when pinching around the top of the bag – this will help prevent the sugarpaste cracking and will ensure that the edges remain smooth.

5 Position the cake on the centre of the cake board. Colour the remaining sugarpaste yellow. Thinly roll out and cut two oblong shapes for the front and the back of the bag. Stick in place with sugar glue, then press different sized orange and pink balls of sugarpaste over the surface, pressing each ball flat.

6 Fill the top of the bag with a variety of colourful sweets, allowing them to spill out of the bag and on to the cake board. If using boiled sweets, bear in mind that these may start to melt slightly, so don't leave the cake too long before serving. Alternatively, keep the pretty wrappers on the sweets.

Cover the cake board with strips of sugarpaste.

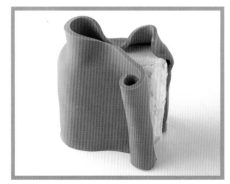
Unroll the pink sugarpaste around the cake.

Press balls of sugarpaste on the sides of the cake.

Little Bo Peep

The story of Little Bo Peep is one of the most popular nursery rhymes ever

MATERIALS

- 2 litre (4 pint/10 cup) bowl-shaped cake, see page 9
- 30cm (12in) round cake board
- 345g (11oz/1⅓ cups) buttercream
- 1.5kg (3lb) sugarpaste/ rolled fondant
- yellow, green, blue, cream & pink food colouring pastes
- icing/confectioners' sugar in a sugar shaker
- 60g (2oz/¼ cup) royal icing
- black food colouring pen

EQUIPMENT

- large rolling pin
- sharp knife
- cake smoother
- templates, see page 109
- 5cm (2in) circle cutter
- cocktail stick/toothpick
- piping bag

USEFUL TIP

Pinch around the front of the base of Little Bo Peep's teardrop-shaped dress to create the edge of the skirt. Place the dress so that it is sitting over the legs.

1 Trim the crust from the cake and slice the top flat. Cut a layer in the cake, then sandwich together with buttercream. Position on the board and spread with buttercream. Colour 1kg (2lb) of sugarpaste yellow-green using green food colouring paste with a touch of yellow. Roll out and cover the cake and board. Smooth around the shape and trim the excess from around the edge. Use a cake smoother to create a smooth surface.

2 To make the bushes, first colour 410g (13oz) of sugarpaste green. Thickly roll out and cut two of each of the bush shapes, using the templates as guides (see page 109). Smooth the edges of the bushes to round off, then position around the base of the cake, securing them in place with dabs of royal icing.

3 Colour 30g (1oz) of sugarpaste blue, 7g (¼oz) cream and 7g (¼oz) yellow. Following the photograph, model Little Bo Peep's dress and shoes. Using cream, model two legs, tapering in at the ankle. Stick in place with royal icing. Roll two tiny balls of white for the socks. Stick the shoes on next. Roll out a piece of white and cut out the apron, using the template (see page 109). Roll a cocktail stick over the surface to thin and frill, then stick on to the dress. Model two white balls for the sleeves, pressing firmly on to the dress and sticking with royal icing. Model a flattened circle and from it cut a 'v' to shape a collar.

4 Roll a ball of cream sugarpaste for Little Bo Peep's head, indenting her mouth with a cocktail stick. Roll a tiny nose and two arms, rounding off the ends for hands. Roll out yellow sugarpaste and cut a circle, then cut in half. Stick in position for the front of her bonnet, smoothing up at the front, then model a flattened ball with the remaining yellow and stick on the back of her head. Roll a long, thin sausage of white and bend to make her crook.

5 Colour 30g (1oz) of sugarpaste pale pink and 7g (¼oz) dark pink. To make the sheep, split the pale pink sugarpaste into five. Model a rounded teardrop for each head, and two teardrop-shaped ears. Indent the bottom of each face with the side of a cocktail stick. Roll dark pink noses. Put the royal icing into the piping bag and cut a small hole in the tip. Stick the sheep in place, peeping out of the bushes, then pipe their hair, swirling the royal icing into curls. When the cake is dry, gently draw on little black dots for eyes.

Sugarpaste shapes for Little Bo Peep.

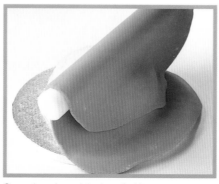

Cover the cake and the board with sugarpaste.

Cut out the bushes, using the templates as a guide.

mouse house

A sweet little pumpkin-shaped mouse house that is quick and easy to make

MATERIALS
- 2 x 2 litre (4 pint/10 cup) bowl-shaped cakes, see page 9
- 30cm (12in) round cake board
- 1.5kg (3lb) sugarpaste/rolled fondant
- mauve, orange, black, golden brown & green food colouring pastes
- icing/confectioners' sugar in a sugar shaker
- 345g (11oz/1⅓ cups) buttercream
- sugar glue

EQUIPMENT
- large rolling pin
- sharp knife
- cake smoother
- small circle cutter

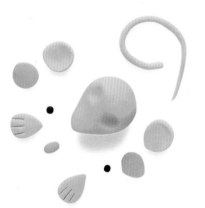

Shapes for the mouse's head, paws and tail.

1 Colour 375g (12oz) of sugarpaste mauve. Using icing sugar to prevent sticking, roll out and cover the cake board, trimming excess from around edge. Put aside to dry. Trim the crust from each cake and slice the tops flat. Put the two cakes together to form a ball.

2 Trim the pumpkin shape, cutting 2cm (¾in) deep into the cake from top to bottom to mark eight sections. Trim to create eight grooves spaced evenly around the cake. Sandwich the cakes together with buttercream, then spread a thin layer over the surface.

3 Colour, then roll out 1kg (2lb) of orange sugarpaste and cover the cake, smoothing around the ball shape and into the grooves. Stretch out the pleats around the base and tuck the sugarpaste underneath, or cut away the pleats and smooth the joins closed.

4 Position the cake on the cake board, then use a cake smoother to smooth the surface. Cut out small circles for the windows and remove the sugarpaste. Colour 15g (½oz) of sugarpaste black, thinly roll out and cut circles to slot in the openings.

5 Colour 45g (1½oz) of sugarpaste golden brown to make the mice. Using 15g (½oz), model a teardrop-shaped head, turning up the point slightly for the muzzle. Indent the eye sockets using your finger, then stick at a window with sugar glue, holding for a moment until secure. Make another mouse head and mark an open mouth with a knife.

6 Model brown, flattened teardrop-shaped ears. Knead orange and golden brown together to make tiny teardrop shapes for the centre of each ear and make small oval-shaped noses. Roll black eyes. Stick in position. Create brown teardrop-shaped paws, flatten slightly, then make three small cuts at the rounded end. Roll tapering shapes for the tails.

7 Colour the remaining sugarpaste green. Roll tapering sausage shapes for the stalks, including a thick stalk for the top of the pumpkin and stick in place. Make flattened leaf shapes, pressing down with your finger to create the leaf edges, then use a knife to mark the centre vein. Model a small sausage of mauve sugarpaste for the base of the chimney and the cone-shaped top, then slot into a hole in the side of the pumpkin house.

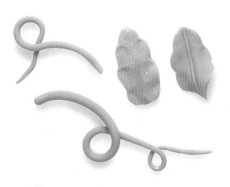

Green sugarpaste stalks and leaves.

Cut eight grooves in the sides of the cake.

Fill the holes with circles of black sugarpaste.

shopping frenzy

Inspired by my daughter, Laura, this is a fun idea for any fashion mad teenage girl

MATERIALS

- 20cm (8in) square cake, see page 8
- 30cm (12in) square cake board
- 315g (10oz/1¼ cups) buttercream
- mauve, purple, pink, aqua, green, yellow, cream & black food colouring pastes
- 1.5kg (3lb) sugarpaste/rolled fondant
- icing/confectioners' sugar in a sugar shaker
- sugar glue
- lengths of liquorice/licorice

EQUIPMENT

- hologram wrapping paper
- non-toxic glue stick
- large rolling pin
- sharp knife
- large heart cutter
- large flower cutter
- cocktail stick/toothpick
- fine paintbrush

1 Cover the cake board with the hologram wrapping paper (see page 7). Trim the crust from the cake and slice the top flat. Cut the cake into four equal squares. Trim each square to taper in at one end. Spread a layer of buttercream over the surface of each cake.

2 Colour 315g (10oz) of sugarpaste mauve, 375g (12oz) purple, 315g (10oz) aqua, 315g (10oz) green, 15g (½oz) yellow and 60g (2oz) cream. Roll out the mauve sugarpaste and cut two 13cm (5in) squares. From the top of each, trim a little handle opening. Place a cake down on to a mauve square and smooth the sides up around the cake. Put the other sugarpaste square on top and glue the joins together.

3 Cover the green bag in the same way, also with cut-out handles. Then make a purple and an aqua bag, without cut-out handles. Position the bags on the cake board. Using 7g (¼oz) of yellow and some of the mauve sugarpaste trimmings, decorate the bags using the heart and flower cutters. Roll two thin sausages of white sugarpaste to make the handles for the aqua bag and stick in place. For the purple bag handles, roll two thin sausages of cream and indent along the length using the side of a cocktail stick to give a rope effect.

4 To make the girl, first colour 45g (1½oz) of sugarpaste dark pink. Make the dress by modelling a teardrop shape, flattening around the base and bending slightly. Using 45g (1½oz) of cream sugarpaste, roll a ball for her head, and stick on to the dress with sugar glue. Position on the cake board, sticking the back of her head against the mauve bag.

5 With the remaining cream sugarpaste, shape two hands and a nose. Push liquorice arms and legs into the dress, using sugar glue to secure. Stick the hands in place. Using 15g (½oz) of purple sugarpaste for each, shape the platform shoes and press on to the legs. Roll long, yellow teardrops for the hair strands. Stick on each side of her head, curling up the ends.

6 Shape purple balls to decorate her dress. Flatten two white balls for eyes and two tiny aqua balls for the iris. Press in the end of a paintbrush to mark the lip centre. Dilute the black and pink food colouring pastes separately with a few drops of water and paint her face. Roll out any trimmings and cut the clothes, folding and sticking them into each bag.

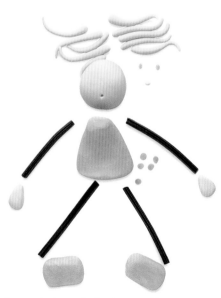
Sugarpaste shapes for the teenage girl.

Cut the cake into four equal squares, then trim.

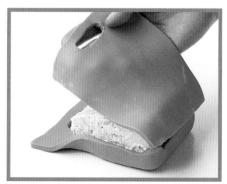
Cover the cake pieces with sugarpaste squares.

football crazy

The chocolate footballs filling the net make this cake a high scorer!

MATERIALS

- 20cm (8in) round cake, see page 8
- 30cm (12in) round cake board
- 410g (13oz/1⅔ cups) buttercream
- 1.125kg (2¼lb) sugarpaste/ rolled fondant
- green, red, cream, black & brown food colouring pastes
- icing/confectioners' sugar in a sugar shaker
- sugar glue
- foil-covered chocolate footballs

EQUIPMENT

- large rolling pin
- sharp knife
- cake smoother
- small circle cutter
- flat-tipped cocktail stick/toothpick
- silver net
- strong adhesive tape

USEFUL TIP

Before securing the silver net to the cake board, add a length of coloured ribbon or any other cake board edging.

1 Trim the crust from the cake and slice the top flat. Split in half and fill with buttercream, then spread a layer of buttercream over the surface of the cake. Scoop out buttercream at the join to create a slight dip. This will prevent a bulge of excess buttercream when the cake is covered with sugarpaste. Position the cake on the centre of the cake board.

2 Colour 1kg (2lb) of sugarpaste green. Roll out, using icing sugar to prevent sticking and cover the cake and board completely, trimming the excess sugarpaste from around the edge of the board with a knife. Smooth the surface with a cake smoother.

3 Using the photograph below as a guide, make the footballer's shorts using 22g (¾oz) of white sugarpaste. Colour 45g (1½oz) of sugarpaste red. Using 35g (1¼oz), make his red top, smoothing out any ridges. Indent his top at the base to hollow it out and then stick over the top of the shorts. Model a flattened circle in white sugarpaste and cut out a 'v' to make a collar. Shape the badge in white sugarpaste, cutting the top with the small circle cutter. Roll two white socks, cutting the end of each straight. Remember that you can alter the footballer's colours to suit a favourite team if you want.

4 Colour 30g (1oz) of sugarpaste cream and use this to make the footballer's head, nose, ears and knees, as well as two sausages for the arms. Pinch around the top of the arms to create a rounded end for the hands, then flatten each hand slightly. Indent the ears with the tip of your finger. Mark his smile using the small circle cutter pressed in at an angle and create dimples at each corner with the end of a cocktail stick.

5 Make the tops of the socks with red, and the sleeve edging with white. Model two oval-shaped eyes. Colour 7g (¼oz) of sugarpaste black. Make the pupils of the eyes, then roll two oval-shaped boots. Colour a small amount of sugarpaste brown and cut into thin strips for the hair. Use the side of a cocktail stick to indent his centre parting.

6 Lay the piece of silver net over the side of the cake. Trim, leaving a 2.5cm (1in) overlap at the edge of the cake board. Secure this overlap underneath the board using strong adhesive tape. Add the foil-covered chocolate balls, putting one in the footballer's hands.

Sugarpaste shapes for the footballer.

Smooth the cake's surface with the cake smoother.

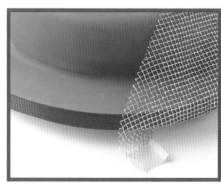
Secure the net under the board with adhesive tape.

busy bees

Busy bees buzzing around their beehive make an unusual birthday cake

MATERIALS
- 1 x 20cm (8in) &
  1 x 15cm (6in) round cakes,
  see page 9
- 25cm (10in) round cake board
- 1.35kg (2¾lb) sugarpaste/
  rolled fondant
- green, yellow & black
  food colouring pastes
- icing/confectioners' sugar
  in a sugar shaker
- 440g (14oz/1¾ cups) buttercream
- sugar glue

EQUIPMENT
- large rolling pin
- sharp knife
- small circle cutter
- small rose petal cutter
- large daisy cutter

USEFUL TIP
*When a large piece
of sugarpaste is rolled out,
lift by folding over the
rolling pin. This will make
it easier to position the
sugarpaste on the cake.*

1 Colour 315g (10oz) of sugarpaste green. Using icing sugar to prevent sticking, roll out and cover the cake board, trimming any excess from around the edge, then put aside to dry. Trim the crust from both cakes and slice the tops flat.

2 Cut a layer in the larger cake, then trim both layers to round off the edges, trimming more from one to make it smaller than the other. Trim the smaller cake in the same way then, using buttercream, sandwich one on top of the other, graduating in size to make the beehive shape. Cut out a wedge of cake from the base for the door. Spread a layer of buttercream over the surface of all the cakes to help the sugarpaste stick.

3 Colour 1kg (2lb) of sugarpaste yellow. Using 30g (1oz), pad the top of the cake to make it dome shaped. Roll out 875g (1¾lb) of yellow sugarpaste and cover the cake completely, smoothing around the shape, stretching out pleats and smoothing downwards. Trim the excess from around the base and position on the centre of the cake board.

4 Reserve a little yellow sugarpaste for the flower centres, then roll the remaining yellow into oval shapes for the bees. Stick the bees over the beehive using sugar glue. Indent little smiles by pressing the circle cutter in at an angle.

5 Colour some of the yellow sugarpaste trimmings black. Thinly roll out and cut a piece of black to fill the doorway, then cut black strips for the bee stripes. Roll tiny black eyes, then stick everything in place with sugar glue.

6 Thinly roll out a piece of white sugarpaste and cut out petal shapes for the bees' wings, using the small rose petal cutter. Stick two wings in place on each bee, positioning the wings just behind the first black stripe.

7 Cut out five daisy shapes using the large daisy cutter and press in the centre of each to indent. Stick the daisies on to the cake board, around the base of the beehive, then stick a small flattened ball of yellow sugarpaste into the centre of each daisy.

Sugarpaste shapes for the bees.

Sandwich the cakes together with buttercream.

Cut out the daisy shapes using the cutter.

building blocks

A rag doll and number building blocks are one way of learning to count

MATERIALS
- 2 x 15cm (6in) square cakes, see page 8
- 30cm (12in) round cake board
- pink & cream food colouring pastes
- 1.75kg (3½lb) sugarpaste/rolled fondant
- icing/confectioners' sugar in a sugar shaker
- 470g (15oz/1¾ cups) buttercream
- sugar glue
- hundreds and thousands/sprinkles

EQUIPMENT
- large rolling pin
- sharp knife
- medium paintbrush
- 2 cake smoothers
- small circle cutter
- cocktail stick/toothpick

Sugarpaste shapes for the rag doll.

1 Colour 375g (12oz) of sugarpaste pink. Roll out and cover the cake board and put aside to dry. Trim the crust from each cake and slice the tops flat. Cut each cake into four equal sized squares. Sandwich the squares together with buttercream to make four cubes, then spread a layer of buttercream over the surface of each cube. Colour 1.25kg (2½lb) of sugarpaste cream. Roll out a little of the cream sugarpaste, then place one side of a cube down on to it and cut around the shape. Cover all sides of each cube in the same way.

2 Tip the hundreds and thousands on to a plate. Decorate one side of a cube at a time. Moisten the edge of the cube with sugar glue and paint a number in the centre with sugar glue. Press the side of the cube down into the hundreds and thousands. As long as the glue is applied liberally, the hundreds and thousands should stick immediately. Use the cake smoothers to move the cubes around to prevent your fingers from knocking the sweets off. Leave one side of each cube undecorated for the base, then assemble all cubes on the cake board and stick them in place with sugar glue.

3 To make the rag doll, colour 90g (3oz) of sugarpaste dark pink, 15g (½oz) flesh, using a touch each of the pink and cream food colouring pastes, and finally 7g (¼oz) yellow. Using the photograph as a guide, model the dress with 75g (2½oz) of dark pink, pressing the bottom to stretch and frill. With the remaining piece of dark pink, model two oval-shaped shoes, two ball sleeves, a small, flattened circle for the collar and two small bows.

4 Moisten the shoes and collar with sugar glue, then press into the hundreds and thousands. Roll a flesh-coloured sugarpaste sausage and cut in half to make legs. Roll two sausages for arms, shaping rounded ends for hands. Stick everything in place. For the head, roll a flesh-coloured ball, then press in the small circle cutter to indent the smile. To dimple the corners, press in the end of the paintbrush. Model a nose and use hundreds and thousands for eyes.

5 Press small pieces of yellow sugarpaste over the head for the hair. To make the plaits, roll tiny sausages, then press along the edges with a cocktail stick. Stick in place with the bows. Decorate the dress and around the cake board edge with hundreds and thousands. Paint the cheeks with a tiny amount of pink food colouring diluted with a drop of water.

Sandwich the cakes together with buttercream.

Place each cube on the sugarpaste and cut around.

Press each cube into the hundreds and thousands.

dippy dinosaur

*A big, scary dinosaur? Certainly
not – this one has far too silly a grin*

MATERIALS

- 2 litre (4 pint/10 cup) bowl-shaped cake, see page 9
- 30cm (12in) round cake board
- 1.4kg (2lb 13oz) sugarpaste/ rolled fondant
- yellow, blue & black food colouring pastes
- icing/confectioners' sugar in a sugar shaker
- 345g (11oz/1⅓ cups) buttercream
- sugar glue

EQUIPMENT

- large rolling pin
- sharp knife
- cake smoother
- food-safe plastic dowelling
- fine paintbrush

USEFUL TIP
*When a large piece of
sugarpaste is rolled out, lift
by folding over the rolling pin.
This will make it easier to position
the sugarpaste on the cake.*

1 Colour 375g (12oz) of sugarpaste yellow. Using icing sugar to prevent sticking, roll out and cover the cake board. Trim the excess from around the edge and put aside to dry. Trim the crust from the cake and slice the top flat, then turn the cake upside down. Cut a layer in the cake and sandwich the two halves back together with buttercream. Spread a layer of buttercream over the surface of the cake to help the sugarpaste stick.

2 Colour 1kg (2lb) of sugarpaste blue. Roll out 750g (1½lb) of blue and cover the cake completely. Stretch out any pleats and smooth the sugarpaste downwards around the shape of the cake. Trim any excess sugarpaste from around the base and position the cake on the cake board. Rub the surface with a cake smoother to remove any bumps.

3 Roll 90g (3oz) of blue sugarpaste into a sausage to create the dinosaur's neck and push the plastic dowelling through the centre. Pinch around the top of the neck to lengthen and narrow the sugarpaste, then shape the base of the neck to slant up at the back, so that it will sit comfortably on the dinosaur's bowl-shaped body.

4 Roll a ball using 60g (2oz) of blue sugarpaste for the dinosaur's head, then pinch at the front to shape a rounded muzzle. Mark the top of the head by pressing the side of the paintbrush into the centre to indent, then smooth around the eye area with your fingers. Mark a wide smile using a knife, then push the end of the paintbrush into each corner of the smile to dimple, and into the top of the muzzle to indent nostrils.

5 Carefully push the dowelling and neck down into the bowl-shaped body, securing it with sugar glue, then press on the head. Colour a tiny amount of sugarpaste black for the pupils and make the eyes with white sugarpaste. With the trimmings of yellow sugarpaste, model several flattened balls in different sizes to decorate the dinosaur's back.

6 Split the remaining blue sugarpaste in half. With one half, roll a sausage tapering into a point at one end and stick against the back of the dinosaur to create his tail. Split the remaining piece of blue sugarpaste into four and model the teardrop-shaped feet, marking the dinosaur's toes with the side of a paintbrush.

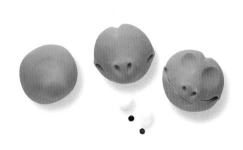
Sugarpaste shapes for the dinosaur's head.

Use the smoother to ensure a perfect finish.

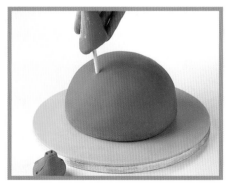
Push the dowelling supporting the neck into the cake.

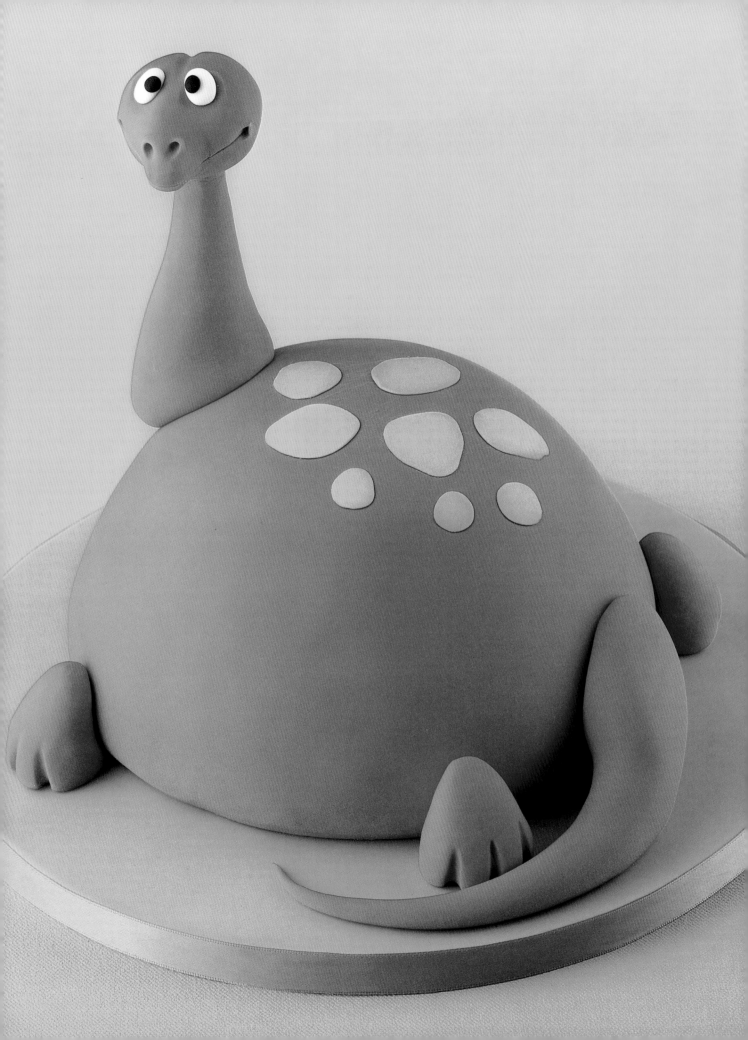

circus clown

A fun, happy clown face is always a popular choice for children's parties

MATERIALS

- 3 litre (6 pint/15 cup) bowl-shaped cake, see page 8
- 35cm (14in) round cake board
- 2kg (4lb) sugarpaste/rolled fondant
- yellow, cream, black, orange, red, blue & green food colouring pastes
- icing/confectioners' sugar in a sugar shaker
- 220g (7oz/1 cup) buttercream
- sugar glue

EQUIPMENT

- large rolling pin
- sharp knife
- cake smoother
- templates, see page 108

USEFUL TIP

Once the clown's face has been covered with sugarpaste, gently rub a cake smoother over the surface.

1 Colour 470g (15oz) of sugarpaste yellow. Using icing sugar to prevent sticking, roll out all the yellow sugarpaste and cover the cake board, trimming any excess from around the edge. Then put the covered cake board aside to dry.

2 Trim the crust from the cake and slice the top flat, using a sharp knife. Spread a layer of buttercream over the surface of the cake to help the sugarpaste stick. Colour 470g (15oz) of sugarpaste cream. Roll out the cream sugarpaste and cover the cake, carefully trimming around the base. Position the cake on the centre of the cake board.

3 Using the templates (see page 108), thinly roll out 45g (1½oz) of white sugarpaste. Cut out the eyes and mouth from this piece. Stick the eyes and mouth in place with sugar glue then, using your finger, smooth a ridge the width of the mouth and indent at each corner to create a smile. Colour 7g (¼oz) of sugarpaste black. Thinly roll out and cut four thin strips for the eyes. Stick the strips in place with sugar glue.

4 To make the clown's hair, first colour 440g (14oz) of sugarpaste orange. Thickly roll out this orange sugarpaste and cut into strips, each approximately 5–7cm (2–3in) in length. Stick these strips around the clown's face, starting at the sides and building up over the top of his head. Colour 140g (4½oz) of sugarpaste red. Make the clown's nose by rolling 45g (1½oz) of the red sugarpaste into a ball, and pressing in place.

5 Colour 250g (8oz) of sugarpaste blue. Roll out and cut the hat rim using the template (see page 108). Using 75g (2½oz) of the blue sugarpaste, roll a ball for the top of the hat. Using red sugarpaste, roll out and cut a thin strip for the hat band and press a small ball flat for the flower centre. Model small teardrop shapes with the yellow trimmings and press flat to make the petals. Using sugar glue, assemble on the clown's head.

6 Roll out the remaining blue sugarpaste and cut out a collar, measuring about 10 x 2cm (4 x ¾in). Stick in place, curling the edge. Colour the last of the sugarpaste green. Make the green, red and blue juggling balls with the remaining pieces of coloured sugarpaste and stick them in place on the board around the clown's face.

Sugarpaste shapes for the clown's hat.

Stick the clown's eyes and mouth in place.

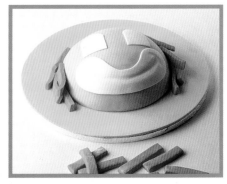

Create the clown's hair with strips of sugarpaste.

camping out

All children love the idea of a sleep-over in their own back garden

MATERIALS
- 20cm (8in) square cake, see page 8
- 30cm (12in) round cake board
- 410g (13oz/1⅔ cups) buttercream
- 1.35kg (2¾lb) sugarpaste/ rolled fondant
- black, blue, navy blue, green, yellow, cream, brown & orange food colouring pastes
- icing/confectioners' sugar in a sugar shaker
- sugar glue

EQUIPMENT
- large rolling pin
- sharp knife
- fork
- small circle cutter
- cocktail stick/toothpick

1 Trim the crust from the cake and slice the top flat. Cut the cake in half and put one half on top of the other. Cut a triangular wedge from either side, cutting down at an outward angle to the base of the first layer. Arrange these two wedges on either side of the cake to create the tent's sloping sides. Trim a dip in the top. Sandwich together with buttercream, then spread buttercream over the surface of the cake. Colour 90g (3oz) of sugarpaste black. Thinly roll out and cut pieces to cover the two ends of the tent.

2 Colour 90g (3oz) dark blue. Thinly roll out and cut four triangular shaped pieces for the inner tent covering, sticking in position with sugar glue. Colour 22g (¾oz) yellow and roll a long, thin sausage for the inner tent trim. Colour 625g (1¼lb) blue. Roll out and cut a piece slightly larger than the cake for the outer tent covering. Roll trimmings into a ball and place at the side to lift up the tent covering for the peeking boy. Lift the sugarpaste and cover the cake.

3 Colour 280g (9oz) of sugarpaste green. Roll out small pieces, position on the cake board and texture by pressing the prongs of a fork over the surface to give a simple grass effect. Colour two pieces of sugarpaste, each weighing 22g (¾oz), navy blue and red. To make the front of the sleeping bags, model two wedges of each colour, sticking one on top of the other at either end. Smooth up at the front to create a space for the heads.

4 Colour 75g (2½oz) of sugarpaste cream, 45g (1½oz) brown, 60g (2oz) pale brown and 7g (¼oz) orange. To make the blonde boy, roll 30g (1oz) of cream into a ball. Indent a smile using the small circle cutter and dimple each corner with a cocktail stick. Shape a cream nose, hands, white eyes and black pupils. Shape flattened pieces of yellow sugarpaste for his hair and arrange on his head, pinching at the front. Make the other boys in this way.

5 Make the dog using the pale brown sugarpaste. Roll two rounded sausages for paws, and stick one on each boy's head. Shape the head, pinching around the centre. Model flattened teardrops for the muzzle, indenting with the tip of a cocktail stick. Flatten teardrop shapes for ears and a tiny piece of dark brown to make the eye patch. Make a black, triangular-shaped nose. Make eyes as before. For the chocolate bar, cut a small square of pale brown and indent using a knife. Put tiny pieces of brown around the boy's mouth.

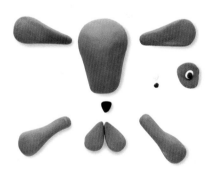

Create the dog's head with pale brown sugarpaste.

Sugarpaste shapes for the little boy's head.

Place the cake wedges cut from the top at the sides.

Cover with buttercream and attach the tent's ends.

pig pen

A fun idea for any pig lover, or perhaps a hint about a teenager's messy bedroom?

MATERIALS

- 25cm (10in) square cake, see page 8
- 20cm (8in) square cake board
- 500g (1lb/2 cups) buttercream
- 1.5kg (3lb) sugarpaste/rolled fondant
- brown, black, yellow, pink & green food colouring pastes
- icing/confectioners' sugar in a sugar shaker
- sugar glue
- 1–2 tsp clear piping gel

EQUIPMENT

- large rolling pin
- sharp knife
- 2.5cm (1in) circle cutter
- cocktail stick/toothpick
- fine grater
- large blossom plunger cutter, see page 5

USEFUL TIP

Instead of colouring the sugarpaste brown, you could use chocolate sugarpaste as a delicious alternative.

1 Trim the crust from the cake and slice the top flat. Cut the cake into four equal sized squares. Trim either side of the two top layers to shape the sloped roof. Sandwich all the layers of cake together with buttercream, then spread a layer of buttercream over the surface of the cake to help the sugarpaste stick.

2 Colour 875g (1¾lb) of sugarpaste brown. Roll out and place one side of the cake down on to it, then cut around the shape. Lift carefully, then mark all the lines for the wooden planks in the brown sugarpaste with a knife. Cover the other side and the front and back of the cake in the same way, sticking the joins together with sugar glue.

3 Mark the plank ends, creating some jagged edges with a knife. Then cut out a little door in the front and a hole in the side of the pen. Remove the sugarpaste from these holes.

4 Colour 375g (12oz) of sugarpaste pale yellow. Roll out and cut an oblong to fit the roof. For the straw effect, make cuts by drawing the knife downwards to stretch and frill the edge, then lift carefully and position on the cake. Mark more lines on the roof and cut a little hole in the front of the roof, removing the sugarpaste.

5 Colour 30g (1oz) of sugarpaste black. Thinly roll out and cut pieces of black sugarpaste to fill the holes in the front, side and roof of the cake. Roll the remaining brown sugarpaste into a strip and cover the cake board around the cake. Press down to mark an uneven surface and trim the excess from the edge.

6 Colour 15g (½oz) of sugarpaste green. Make the blades of grass by rubbing the piece of green sugarpaste over a fine grater. Sprinkle the resulting tiny blades of grass in little piles on the cake board and around the edge of the pig pen, scattering unevenly. Use sugar glue to secure the piles in position.

continued overleaf!

Sugarpaste pieces for the pig's head, ears and snout.

Sandwich the layers of cake with buttercream.

Cut a wooden plank effect with a knife.

Mark a straw roof in the yellow sugarpaste.

Grate green sugarpaste to form blades of grass.

7 Roll out the trimmings of yellow sugarpaste and cut thin strips to scatter as straw around the cake board. To make the blossom, roll out white sugarpaste and cut all the flowers with the blossom plunger cutter (see page 5). Roll little balls of yellow for the centres of the flowers. Spread a little clear piping gel over the cake board to create the mud.

8 Colour 125g (4oz) of sugarpaste pink and 15g (½oz) dark pink. To make a pig's head, roll a ball of pink, then mark a smile using the circle cutter pressed in at an angle. Indent two eyes using the tip of a cocktail stick. Model two triangular-shaped ears in pink sugarpaste, turning them up at the tip. Model an oval-shaped snout using the dark pink sugarpaste, again indenting with the cocktail stick.

9 Make several different sized pigs and stick them in place around the pig pen with sugar glue. For the pig's bottom, mark a line on a ball of pink sugarpaste using a knife. Then roll a thin sausage of paste and twist it round to make a curly tail, and shape two tiny feet. Stick in position outside the door of the pen.

Place the pigs' heads around the pig pen, with two heads peeking out of the holes cut in the roof.

skull & crossbones

Would-be pirates will go goggle-eyed over this skull and crossbones

MATERIALS

- 1 x 20cm (8in) & 1 x 15cm (6in) round cakes, see page 9
- 35cm (14in) square cake board
- 2kg (4lb) sugarpaste/rolled fondant
- black food colouring paste
- icing/confectioners' sugar in a sugar shaker
- 375g (12oz/1½ cups) buttercream

EQUIPMENT

- large rolling pin
- sharp knife
- templates, see page 109

Use black sugarpaste to fill the eyes, nose and mouth.

1 Colour 625g (1¼lb) of sugarpaste black. Using icing sugar to prevent sticking, roll out 500g (1lb) of black sugarpaste and cover the cake board, trimming the excess from around the edge. Put the covered cake board aside to dry.

2 Trim the crust from each cake and slice the tops flat. Cut a 2.5cm (1in) wedge away from the side of each cake, then trim around the top edge of both cakes to round off. Spread the surface of the cakes with buttercream, then position them on the cake board with the two cut edges pressed together.

3 Roll out 1kg (2lb) of white sugarpaste and cover the cake completely, trimming carefully around the base. Using the templates (see page 109), cut out the eyes, nose and mouth from the top of the cake. Thinly roll out black sugarpaste and cut shapes to fill the spaces. Roll two small balls of white sugarpaste for the eyes, then roll out and cut the teeth.

4 To make the bones, roll four thick sausages of white sugarpaste, keeping a rounded end on each. Make a small cut in each rounded end and smooth to remove ridges, then position on the cake board at the sides of the skull.

little blue train

This bright train brimming with sweets will chug on to the birthday party table

MATERIALS
- 18cm (7in) square cake, see page 8
- 30cm (12in) hexagonal cake board
- 1.5kg (3lb) sugarpaste/ rolled fondant
- pink, blue & black food colouring pastes
- icing/confectioners' sugar in a sugar shaker
- sugar glue
- 440g (14oz/1¾ cups) buttercream
- length of liquorice/licorice
- liquorice catherine wheels/ licorice wheels
- assorted liquorice/licorice candies

EQUIPMENT
- large rolling pin
- sharp knife

USEFUL TIP
Gently rub the surface of the sugarpaste with your hands to remove excess icing sugar and give a sheen.

1 Colour 500g (1lb) of sugarpaste pink. Using icing sugar to prevent sticking, roll out the pink sugarpaste and use it to cover the cake board, trimming any excess from around the edge. Put the covered cake board aside to dry.

2 Trim the crust from the cake and slice the top flat, using a sharp knife. Cut a strip measuring 8cm (3in) from one side of the cake. Cut this slice into two pieces, one 7cm (2½in) long and the other 10cm (4in) long. Put the larger piece upright at the end of the smaller piece to form the engine. Trim a curve in the top of the larger piece. Cut the remaining cake into three equal pieces to make the carriages.

3 Sandwich the engine together with buttercream, then spread a layer of buttercream over all the cakes to help the sugarpaste stick. Colour 875g (1¾lb) of sugarpaste blue. Roll out 375g (12oz) of the blue sugarpaste and use to cover the engine completely, smoothing down and around the shape, trimming any excess from around the base. Cover the three carriages in the same way, using the leftover blue sugarpaste.

4 Colour the remaining sugarpaste black. Roll out and cut an oblong that will fit the top of the engine, sticking in place with sugar glue. Thinly roll out black sugarpaste and cut four strips for the windows and stick them in place, then model two flattened ball shapes for the pupils of the eyes and put to one side.

5 Cut three small lengths of liquorice to link the carriages and engine together and put aside. Position all the liquorice 'wheels' against the engine and carriages using a tiny amount of sugarpaste moistened with sugar glue to stick them in place.

6 Carefully place the engine and carriages on the covered cake board and link them together using the lengths of liquorice put aside earlier. Decorate the engine with the assorted liquorice candies and pile candies on to the top of each carriage, securing in place with sugar glue. Use two square pieces of liquorice to form the train's eyes, sticking on the black sugarpaste pupils made earlier.

Cut the cake into five pieces to create the train.

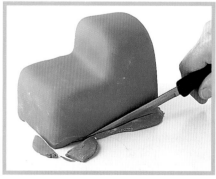
Cover the engine with blue sugarpaste and trim.

Place the liquorice wheels on the side of the train.

hungry bookworm

A cake for avid readers, or perhaps a subtle hint to someone who does not read enough

MATERIALS
- 18cm (7in) square cake, see page 8
- 30cm (12in) square cake board
- 1.25kg (2½lb) sugarpaste/rolled fondant
- green, blue, yellow, black & orange food colouring pastes
- icing/confectioners' sugar in a sugar shaker
- 375g (12oz/1½ cups) buttercream
- sugar glue

EQUIPMENT
- large rolling pin
- sharp knife
- cake smoother
- 1cm (½in), 2cm (¾in) & 4cm (1½in) circle cutters
- length of raw spaghetti

USEFUL TIP
A special birthday message can be added to the cake to look like the title of the book.

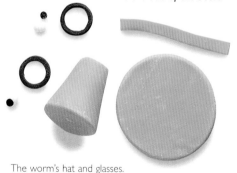

The worm's hat and glasses.

1 Colour, then roll out 440g (14oz) of green sugarpaste and cover the cake board. Put aside to dry, reserving the trimmings from around the edge of the cake board. Trim the crust from the cake and slice the top flat. Cut away 2.5cm (1in) from one side of the cake to make an oblong book shape. Cut a layer in the cake and sandwich together with buttercream, then spread a layer of buttercream over the surface of the cake.

2 Position the cake on the cake board. Roll out 220g (7oz) of white sugarpaste and cut a strip to fit around three sides of the cake, leaving the book bind edge uncovered. Mark all the page lines in the white sugarpaste with the back of a knife.

3 Colour, then roll out 410g (13oz) of blue sugarpaste and cut a piece slightly larger than the top of the cake and the book bind edge. Position on the cake, using the cake smoother to create a smooth surface. Cut a strip from the trimmings to fit around the base of the cake, securing it with sugar glue. Remove two circles of sugarpaste from the top. Colour, then thinly roll out 7g (¼oz) of black sugarpaste and cut circles to fill the spaces.

4 Colour 75g (2½oz) of sugarpaste yellow to make the worm. Using 60g (2oz), model a fat teardrop shape for the worm's head. Indent the smile by pressing the 2cm (¾in) circle cutter in at an angle. Push a 10cm (4in) length of raw spaghetti into the large hole, down to the base of the cake to support the worm's head. Moisten with sugar glue, then carefully push the head in position on the spaghetti. Roll the remaining yellow into a sausage tapering in at one end and stick in position coming out of the smaller hole.

5 Roll out the green trimmings. Cut a circle for the hat rim with the large cutter and put it aside to set, then model the top of the hat. Put aside two tiny balls of white for the eyes, then colour the remaining sugarpaste orange. Roll out and cut a strip for the hat.

6 Model two flattened balls of black sugarpaste and cut out the centre of each using the smallest circle cutter. Leave to set for at least ten minutes, then stick in place as the worm's glasses. Roll two white balls for the eyes and two tiny black balls for the pupils. Thinly roll out the orange sugarpaste and cut strips to edge the cake and board.

Mark pages using the back of a knife.

Place a strip of blue sugarpaste around the base.

Push the worm's head on to the piece of spaghetti.

baby in a pram

A baby doll and teddy in their own pram make the perfect cake for small girls

MATERIALS
- 2 litre (4 pint/10 cup) bowl-shaped cake, see page 9
- 25cm (10in) petal-shaped cake board
- mauve, pink, cream & yellow food colouring pastes
- 1.75kg (3½lb) sugarpaste/ rolled fondant
- icing/confectioners' sugar in a sugar shaker
- 375g (12oz/1½ cups) buttercream
- sugar glue
- length of fondant-filled liquorice/licorice
- 4 liquorice/ licorice wheels

EQUIPMENT
- large rolling pin
- sharp knife
- miniature, 1.5cm (¾in) & 13cm (5in) circle cutters
- cocktail stick/toothpick

1 Colour 375g (12oz) of sugarpaste mauve. Using icing sugar to prevent sticking, roll out 315g (10oz) and cover the cake board completely, trimming any excess from around the edge and put aside to dry. Trim the crust from the cake and slice the top flat. Cut two layers in the cake and sandwich back together with buttercream.

2 Colour 1kg (2lb) of sugarpaste pink. Roll a sausage using 140g (4½oz) and place around the top edge of the cake to create a lip. Turn the cake upside down. Roll out 750g (1½lb) of pink sugarpaste and use to cover the cake completely, stretching out pleats and smoothing the sugarpaste around the shape of the cake. Turn the cake over, then smooth the sugarpaste inside the lip, trimming away excess. Position the cake on the cake board.

3 Roll out 75g (2½oz) of white sugarpaste. Cut a circle to cover the top of the cake using the large circle cutter. Shape a pillow using 125g (4oz) of white. Put aside a tiny amount of pink for the teddy's nose, then roll the remaining pink into two sausages tapering at either end and stick in position, one on top of the other, for the pram hood. Bend the liquorice stick and push in for the handle. Stick the liquorice wheels in place with sugar glue.

4 Colour 90g (3oz) of sugarpaste cream and 75g (2½oz) pale yellow. Roll a small ball nose and the doll's head with the cream sugarpaste. Indent facial features by pressing the circle cutters in at an angle. Dimple the doll's smile by pressing in each corner with the tip of a cocktail stick. Mark eyelashes with the tip of a knife. With a small piece of pale yellow sugarpaste, roll a long teardrop and twist to make the curly hair.

5 Roll 22g (¾oz) of mauve sugarpaste into a ball for the teddy's head. With 7g (¼oz), model a flattened oval muzzle, two sausage shapes for arms and two ball ears. Indent the muzzle using a knife and indent the smile. Press a cocktail stick into each ear to indent, then stick the ears in place. Press in the tip to mark eyes. Model the pink triangular nose.

6 Roll out the remaining pale yellow and cut a circle using the large circle cutter. Press to create a scalloped edge, then fold and place in the pram. Thinly roll out the remaining mauve sugarpaste and cut circles to stick over the pram using the 1.5cm (¾in) circle cutter.

Create a lip with a sausage of pink sugarpaste.

Smooth the sugarpaste around and inside the lip.

Mark the doll's eyelashes with the tip of a knife.

pony stable

This pretty stable and ponies will bring a sparkle to any little girl's special day

MATERIALS
- 20cm (8in) square cake, see page 8
- 30cm (12in) petal-shaped cake board
- 1.25kg (2½lb) sugarpaste/rolled fondant
- blue, green, yellow, black & pink food colouring pastes
- icing/confectioners' sugar in a sugar shaker
- 345g (11oz/1⅓ cups) buttercream
- sugar glue
- silver dragees

EQUIPMENT
- large rolling pin
- sharp knife
- large & small flower cutters
- small pieces of foam sponge
- small circle cutter
- cocktail stick/toothpick
- 3 x 2.5cm (1in) lengths of raw spaghetti
- bone tool, illustrated overleaf

USEFUL TIP
When the flower shape is in the cutter, rub the edge of the cutter to remove excess sugarpaste and create a clean edge.

1 Colour 410g (13oz) of sugarpaste turquoise with the blue and green food colouring pastes. Using icing sugar to prevent sticking, roll out 375g (12oz) and cover the cake board, trimming excess from around the edge, then put aside to dry.

2 Trim the crust from the cake and slice the top flat. Cut the cake exactly in half and put one half on top of the other. Cut a sloping roof, cutting down to the bottom of the top layer with a sharp knife. Sandwich together with buttercream, then spread a layer of buttercream over the surface of the cake to help the sugarpaste stick.

3 Roll out 750g (1½lb) of white sugarpaste and put the end of the stable down on to it. Cut around the shape. Put the cake down on its base and, using a knife, mark lines in the sugarpaste to create a wood effect. Cover the opposite end of the cake, then the back, and finally the front in the same way, before positioning the cake on the cake board.

4 Cut out three windows at the front of the stable, removing the sugarpaste. Colour 22g (¾oz) of sugarpaste dark turquoise. Thinly roll out and cut pieces to fill the spaces.

5 To make the flower-shaped roof tiles, knead turquoise and white sugarpaste together until streaky. Roll out and cut out all the flower shapes with the large flower cutter. Stick the flowers over the roof with sugar glue, starting at the base and working upwards.

6 Create door handles by modelling little loops using the dark turquoise sugarpaste trimmings. Stick the handles and a silver dragee in place on each door with sugar glue.

7 To make the ponies, first colour 30g (1oz) of sugarpaste pale yellow, 22g (¾oz) pink and 15g (½oz) grey. To make the yellow pony, roll 15g (½oz) of yellow into a smooth, crack-free ball, then pinch all the way round to shape the pony's muzzle, pressing gently to keep a smooth surface and pulling it to lengthen, then round off the end.

continued overleaf/

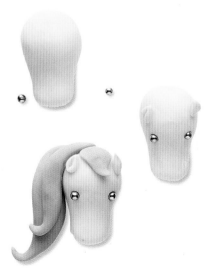

Sugarpaste shapes for the pony's head and mane.

Sandwich the cake together with buttercream.

Place the cake on the sugarpaste and cut to fit.

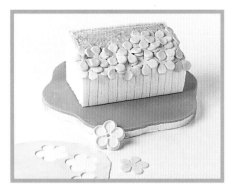

Cut flowers using the large flower cutter.

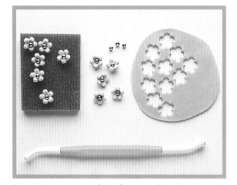

Indent the centres of the flowers with a bone tool.

8 Insert a length of raw spaghetti into one of the windows on the front of the cake and moisten the area with sugar glue. Carefully push the pony's head in place, using a piece of foam sponge for support while it is drying. Indent a smile by pressing in the circle cutter at an angle, and indent nostrils with the tip of a cocktail stick.

9 For the mane, shape the remaining turquoise sugarpaste into different sized sausages, tapering to a point at either end and stick in place. Curl up the ends, then flatten a small teardrop shape for the forelock. Model tiny ears, indenting the centre of each with a cocktail stick. Carefully press in silver dragees for eyes.

10 Model the other two ponies in the same way. Make all the small flowers using the small flower cutter and the remaining pink and yellow sugarpaste. Indent the centre of each flower with the end of a bone tool, and stick in a silver dragee to decorate. Stick the small pink and yellow flowers over the cake board and the stable roof using sugar glue.

11 Leave the finished cake to dry completely before carefully removing the pieces of foam sponge used to support the ponies' heads.

Decorative silver dragees for the ponies' eyes and in the centre of the flowers add a sparkle to this pretty cake.

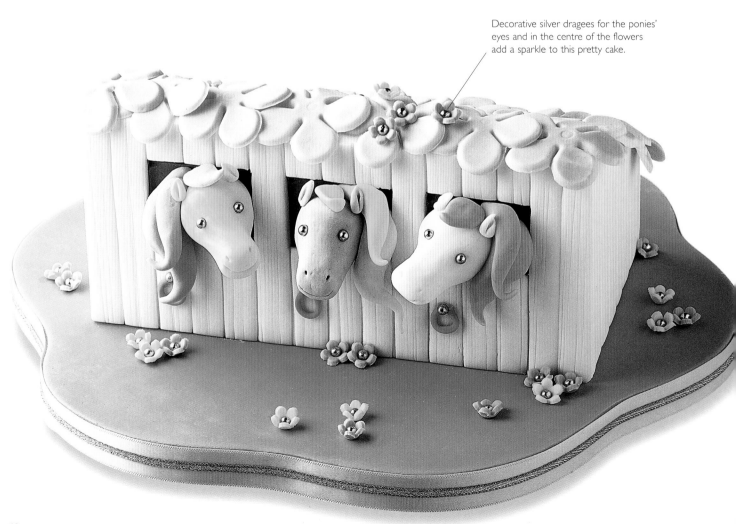

treasure map

Pirate treasure can easily be found with chocolate gold coins shining everywhere

MATERIALS
- 20cm (8in) round cake, see page 8
- 30cm (12in) round cake board
- 410g (13oz/1⅔ cups) buttercream
- 1kg (2lb) sugarpaste/ rolled fondant
- golden brown & blue food colouring pastes
- icing/confectioners' sugar in a sugar shaker
- light brown sugar
- foil-covered chocolate coins
- black food colouring pen
- edible gold sparkle powder/ petal dust/blossom tint

EQUIPMENT
- large rolling pin
- sharp knife
- gold embroidery thread
- medium paintbrush

1 Trim the crust from the cake and slice the top flat. Split the cake in two and sandwich together with buttercream, then position on the cake board. Spread a layer of buttercream over the surface of the cake to help the sugarpaste stick.

2 Colour 875g (1¾lb) of sugarpaste golden brown. Using icing sugar to prevent sticking, roll out and cover the cake and the board completely, smoothing the sugarpaste around the shape of the cake. Trim the excess from around the cake board edge. Place a length of gold embroidery thread over the top of the cake.

3 Colour the remaining sugarpaste cream using a tiny amount of golden brown food colouring. Thinly roll out and cut an 18cm (7in) square to create the treasure map. Make different sized cuts along the top and bottom edge. Roll up one side of the map and position on the cake. Arrange the gold thread ends over the map.

4 Sprinkle some light brown sugar around the cake and position all the gold coins. Leave the cake to dry, then draw on the map using the black food colouring pen and paint with diluted blue and golden brown food colouring pastes. Finally, brush the cake with the gold sparkle powder.

castle guards

Look-out guards will have to be extra vigilant or this cake will soon disappear

MATERIALS
- 25cm (10in) square cake, see page 8
- 12 mini swiss rolls/jelly rolls
- 25cm (10in) round cake board
- 440g (14oz/1¾ cups) buttercream
- 1.5kg (3lb) sugarpaste/ rolled fondant
- black, cream & green food colouring pastes
- icing/confectioners' sugar in a sugar shaker
- sugar glue

EQUIPMENT
- small rolling pin
- sharp knife
- 3.5cm (1½in) circle cutter
- small square cutter
- cocktail stick/toothpick

Cut the turrets using the square cutter.

1 Trim the crust from the cake and slice the top flat. Cut the cake into four equal squares and sandwich the squares together with buttercream to form the castle. Sandwich three mini swiss rolls together for each corner tower, then spread a layer of buttercream over the surface of the entire cake to help the sugarpaste stick.

2 Colour 125g (4oz) of sugarpaste black. Using icing sugar to prevent sticking, thinly roll out 60g (2oz) and cut a panel to cover the front of the cake. Colour 250g (8oz) of sugarpaste pale grey, 625g (1¼lb) grey and 250g (8oz) dark grey using a touch of black food colouring paste. Roll out 155g (5oz) of grey sugarpaste and cut a square to cover the top of the cake, then cut four circles using the cutter and position one on top of each tower. Using the different shades of grey, shape flattened pieces of sugarpaste and press on to the cake surface, covering the cake completely, apart from three windows and a doorway at the front.

3 With the remaining grey sugarpaste, roll out and cut strips measuring 2.5cm (1in) in depth. Cut the turrets using the small square cutter and stick in place with sugar glue. Thinly roll out and cut strips for the portcullis, indenting with the tip of a cocktail stick. Slightly flatten small modelled balls of grey sugarpaste to create an edging for the doorway.

4 Split 7g (¼oz) of dark grey sugarpaste into three pieces and model teardrop shapes for the guards' helmets. Stick these with the point uppermost at each window, then press to indent the centre of each. Colour a small amount of sugarpaste cream and model three ball-shaped heads and oval-shaped noses and hands, sticking in place with sugar glue. Mark the faces with a cocktail stick. Shape tiny sleeves with grey sugarpaste.

5 Shape the cannon with 30g (1oz) of black sugarpaste by rolling a ball, then pinching to shape the funnel. Push a cocktail stick into the end and twist around to open up. With the remaining black, model flattened circles for wheels and roll the cannon balls.

6 Colour the remaining sugarpaste green. Roll out and press on to the cake board, pushing up against the cake and indenting with the rolling pin to mark an uneven surface. With the remaining pieces of grey, shape rocks and scatter them over the board.

Sandwich the cake and swiss rolls with buttercream.

Place a panel of black sugarpaste on the front.

Cover the cake with flattened pieces of sugarpaste.

toy boat

A simply shaped boat that all pre-school children will love

MATERIALS
- 2 litre (4 pint/10 cup) bowl-shaped cake, see page 9
- 25cm (10in) round cake board
- 1.75kg (3½lb) sugarpaste/ rolled fondant
- blue, red, yellow, black & green food colouring pastes
- icing/confectioners' sugar in a sugar shaker
- 345g (11oz/1⅓ cups) buttercream
- sugar glue

EQUIPMENT
- large rolling pin
- sharp knife
- small & medium bowls
- cake smoother
- small & medium circle cutters
- cocktail stick/toothpick

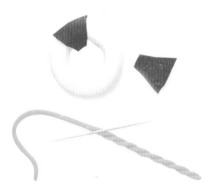

Sugarpaste shapes for the lifebelts and rope.

1 Colour 315g (10oz) of sugarpaste blue. Using icing sugar to prevent sticking, roll out and cover the cake board completely, trimming excess from around edge. To indent water ripples, firmly press down the rim of the two bowls several times into the sugarpaste covering.

2 Trim the cake crust and slice the top flat. Cut a layer from the top measuring 1cm (½in) in depth. Cut into squares and stack together to make the cabin. Trim so the stack tapers in at the base, then sandwich together with buttercream. Spread the surface with buttercream.

3 Turn the cake upside down. Cut a wedge off one end to form the back of the boat, then cut wedges from either side to shape the sides of the boat so they form a point at the front. Turn the cake over and spread a layer of buttercream over the surface.

4 Colour 1kg (2lb) of sugarpaste red. Roll a long sausage and position it around the top of the boat to create a lip. Roll out 875g (1¾lb) of red sugarpaste and cover the cake, smoothing around the shape. Smooth the sugarpaste and trim. Position the boat on the cake board and smooth the surface with a cake smoother.

5 Colour, then roll out 155g (5oz) of yellow sugarpaste. Cover each side of the cabin separately by putting the cake down on the sugarpaste and cutting around, then smooth the joins closed. Remove a circle of sugarpaste for each porthole. Colour, then roll out 7g (¼oz) of black sugarpaste thinly, and cut circles to slot in the spaces. Stick the cabin on the boat. Colour 125g (4oz) of sugarpaste green. Roll out 45g (1½oz) and cut a square to fit the roof.

6 Roll the remaining green and red separately into two balls. Stick the two together, and roll over the work surface into a teardrop shape using the cake smoother. Cut at either end to create a straight edge and stick in position on top of the cabin to form the funnel.

7 Roll out white sugarpaste and cut five circles using the larger circle cutter. Cut a smaller circle from the centre. Stick against the side of the boat. Roll out red sugarpaste and cut two triangles for each lifebelt. Roll thin sausages of yellow sugarpaste. Press with a cocktail stick at intervals to create a rope effect. Cut into lengths and stick between each lifebelt.

Stack layers of cake to form the boat's cabin.

Create a lip with a length of red sugarpaste.

Make portholes with circles of black sugarpaste.

candy house

Absolutely covered in sweets –
this has to be a child's dream come true

MATERIALS

- 25cm (10in) square cake, see page 8
- 25cm (10in) round cake board
- 1.5kg (3lb) sugarpaste/ rolled fondant
- green, yellow & pink food colouring pastes
- icing/confectioners' sugar in a sugar shaker
- 500g (1lb/2 cups) buttercream
- sugar glue
- assorted sweets/candies
- lollipops
- hundreds and thousands/sprinkles
- vermicelli/sugar strands

EQUIPMENT

- large rolling pin
- sharp knife
- cake smoother
- 3cm (1¼in) circle cutter

USEFUL TIP

Use any types of sweets available to decorate this simple house. As a special treat, use your child's favourite sweets.

1 Colour 440g (14oz) of sugarpaste green. Using icing sugar to prevent sticking, roll out 315g (10oz) and cover the cake board, trimming the excess sugarpaste from around the edge. Put the covered cake board aside to dry.

2 Trim the crust from the cake and slice the top flat. Cut the cake into four equal squares. Put one on top of the other, making sure that each layer sits straight. Trim a wedge from either side of the two top layers of cake to create the sloping roof.

3 Sandwich all the layers of cake together using buttercream, then spread a layer of buttercream over the surface of the cake to help the sugarpaste stick.

4 Colour 1kg (2lb) of sugarpaste pale yellow. Split 22g (¾oz) in half, roll into balls and press on to the front of the house to create padding for the cheeks. Roll out 170g (5½oz) of pale yellow sugarpaste and cut two pieces to cover the two sides of the house. Press in position and smooth with a cake smoother.

5 Roll out 220g (7oz) of yellow sugarpaste. Position the back of the cake down on to this piece of yellow sugarpaste and cut around the shape. Repeat this process to cover the front of the cake. Carefully position the covered cake on the cake board. Sugar glue the joins and smooth them closed. Using your finger, gently indent the smile.

6 Roll out the remaining pale yellow sugarpaste and cut a piece slightly larger than the two sides of the roof. Position this on top of the cake. Moisten the roof with sugar glue. Arrange some of the smaller, soft sweets over the roof, covering it completely.

7 Using the remaining green sugarpaste, model some bushes around the base of the house, positioning them where the lollipops will be. Moisten the lollipop sticks and push them into the bushes for support. For large lollipops, moisten a tiny amount of sugarpaste with sugar glue and use to stick the top of the lollipop against the house more securely.

continued overleaf!

Create eyes with sweets and sugarpaste shapes.

Trim the top layers of the cake to create the roof.

Cut around the shape of the cake with a knife.

Stick the sweets to the roof with sugar glue.

8 Arrange all the remaining sweets around the cake board, piling against the sides of the house. Moisten the front path with sugar glue, then sprinkle with hundreds and thousands which will stick to the glue. Sprinkle the bushes with sugar strands.

9 Thinly roll out 7g (¼oz) of white sugarpaste and cut a circle. Cut the circle in half for the eyes. Cut strips for the top and bottom using pale yellow trimmings. Stick on to the house using two sweets for the pupils and a sprinkling of sugar strands for the eyelashes.

10 Colour the remaining sugarpaste pink. Thinly roll out and cut an oblong for the door. Using the circle cutter, cut a curve in the top, then stick in place on the front of the cake. Use hundreds and thousands for a tiny door handle.

Sprinkle the green bushes supporting the lollipops with sugar strands.

flower power

Certainly eyecatching, this trendy flower cake is a treat for any teenager

MATERIALS

- 20cm (8in) petal-shaped cake, see page 8
- 30cm (12in) round cake board
- 410g (13oz/1½ cups) buttercream
- icing/confectioners' sugar in a sugar shaker
- 1kg (2lb) sugarpaste/rolled fondant
- orange, yellow & black food colouring pastes
- sheet of rice paper
- black, yellow, orange, pink, blue & green food colouring pens
- sugar glue
- small length of liquorice/licorice

EQUIPMENT

- sheet of flower print wrapping paper
- non-toxic glue stick
- sheet of greaseproof paper/ wax baking paper
- scissors
- large rolling pin
- sharp knife
- cake smoother
- templates, see page 108
- 5cm (2in) & miniature circle cutters
- cocktail stick/toothpick
- small pieces of foam sponge

1 Cover the cake board with paper, as described on page 7. Cut out the cake shape in greaseproof paper using the bakeware as a guide. This act as a barrier between the cake and the paper-covered cake board. Trim the crust from the cake and slice the top flat. Cut a layer in the cake and sandwich together using buttercream. Spread a thin layer of buttercream over the cake. Roll out 750g (1½lb) of white sugarpaste and cover the cake.

2 Colour 250g (8oz) of sugarpaste orange. Roll out and cut six petals, using the template (see page 108). Smooth the edges of each to round off, then stick in place around the cake with sugar glue. Cut out a circle in the centre and remove the sugarpaste. Colour the white trimmings yellow and cut out a flattened ball to fill the centre of the cake.

3 Cut out the butterfly's wings from a piece of rice paper using the template (see page 108). With the black food colouring pen, draw the pattern on each wing on the smooth side of the rice paper. Colour the design using the food colouring pens, then put aside to dry.

4 Colour 7g (¼oz) of the trimmings black. Roll a long teardrop shape for the butterfly's body, then roll a ball-shaped head, two pupils and two balls for the end of each antenna. Press the tiny circle cutter into the head to indent the smile. Using a cocktail stick, make two tiny holes in the top of the butterfly's head. Cut two tiny strips of liquorice and slot into the holes, securing with sugar glue. Stick the two balls on the top of each antenna. Using a tiny amount of white sugarpaste, make the eyes, sticking the black pupils in place.

5 To assemble the butterfly, stick the body and head on the cake. With a knife, make two cuts either side of the body. Moisten with sugar glue and slot in the rice paper wings. Cut strips of rice paper to fit each curve of the cake. Colour the strips different colours. Moisten with sugar glue and stick around the cake.

Paint the butterfly's wings with food colouring pens.

formula 1 car

Any car-mad racing fan will be unstoppable when they see this winner

MATERIALS
- 25cm (10in) square cake, see page 8
- 35cm (14in) round cake board
- 2kg (4lb) sugarpaste/ rolled fondant
- black, red, blue & green food colouring pastes
- icing/confectioners' sugar in a sugar shaker
- sugar glue
- 375g (12oz/1½ cups) buttercream

EQUIPMENT
- large rolling pin
- sharp knife
- cake smoother
- number cutter
- templates, see page 110

USEFUL TIP
Use food colouring pens if you want to add more detailing to the car. Available in a range of colours, these pens are perfect for drawing fine lines and writing on sugarpaste. Before you start, make sure that the cake is completely dry.

1 Colour 410g (13oz) of sugarpaste grey, using a touch of black food colouring paste, then colour 75g (2½oz) of sugarpaste red. Roll out the grey and cover the cake board, leaving a section uncovered on one side. Trim this side into a curve. Roll out and cut red and white sugarpaste strips and stick on the board to fill the gap, using sugar glue, then put aside to dry.

2 Trim the crust from the cake and slice the top flat. Cut the cake in half. One half is the main body of the cake. Trim either side at the front to taper in and trim to slope down. Cut a wedge measuring 5cm (2in) from the other half and use to lengthen the cake. Cut another wedge measuring 4cm (1½in) to heighten the back of the cake. From the remaining cake, cut two pieces for either side of the car.

3 Using buttercream, sandwich all the pieces of cake together, then spread a layer of buttercream over the surface of the cake. Colour 875g (1¾lb) of sugarpaste blue. To create the driving seat, roll a ball using 30g (1oz) of blue and press just in front of the raised wedge. Roll a sausage with 15g (½oz) and position in a curve on top of the cake.

4 Roll out the remaining blue and cover the cake completely, smoothing around the shape and into the grooves. Trim around the base, being careful not to mark the cake board. Roll out 75g (2½oz) of white sugarpaste and cut a wedge for the top of the back of the car, then cut two side pieces using the template (see page 110), sticking in place with sugar glue.

5 Colour 75g (2½oz) of sugarpaste green. Using the templates (see page 110), cut wedges for the front of the car at either side, then cut two side pieces. Stick in place. Roll a ball using 45g (1½oz) of green to make the driver's helmet and stick on to the top of the cake.

6 To make the tyres, first colour 375g (12oz) black. Split 345g (11oz) of this black sugarpaste into four equal sized pieces. Roll one of the pieces into a ball, then press down gently with the cake smoother to flatten. Make the three other tyres in the same way and stick in place with sugar glue. Using the remaining sugarpaste, thinly roll out and cut pieces to decorate the car, using the templates (see page 110) and a number cutter relevant to the birthday. Cut a small strip for the helmet visor using black sugarpaste.

Place the shaped cakes together to form the car.

Create the driving seat with sugarpaste shapes.

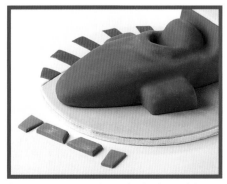

Cut green sugarpaste shapes for the front of the car.

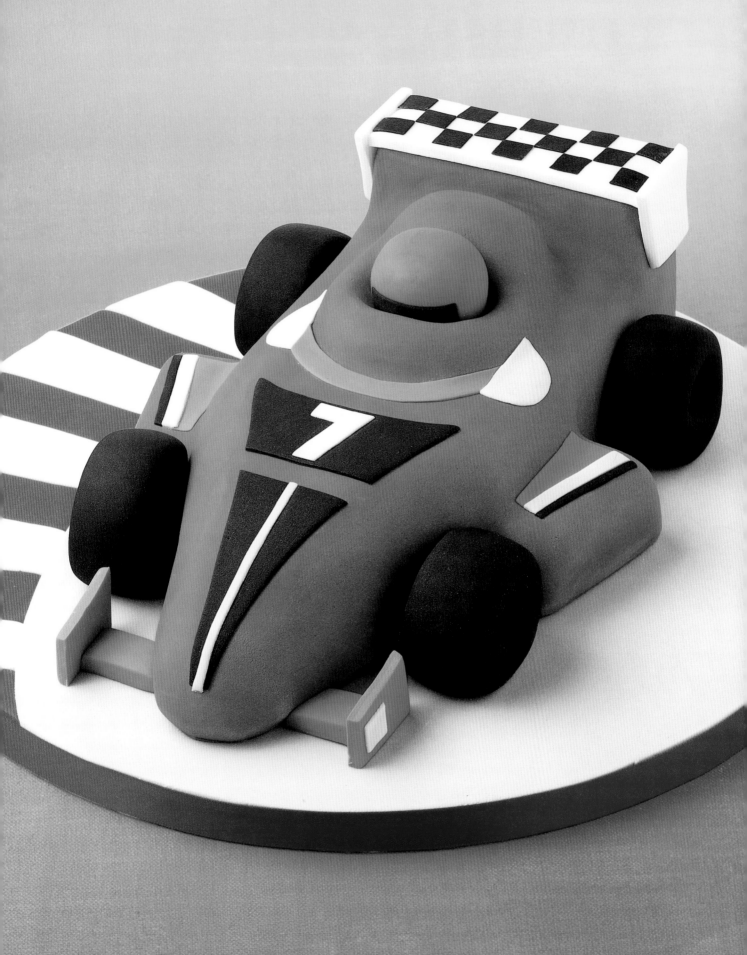

crowning glory

This jewelled crown is sure to be the centre of attention at any party

MATERIALS

- 20cm (8in) round cake, see page 8
- 20cm (8in) round cake board
- 375g (12oz/1½ cups) buttercream
- 1.25kg (2½lb) sugarpaste/rolled fondant
- icing/confectioners' sugar in a sugar shaker
- red food colouring paste
- 155g (5oz/⅔ cup) royal icing
- fruit-flavoured sweets/candies

EQUIPMENT

- large rolling pin
- sharp knife
- gold card
- scissors
- templates, see page 108
- piping bag

USEFUL TIP

If you would like to add ribbon banding to the edge of the cake board, apply before decorating the cake sides.

1 Trim the crust from the cake, keeping the top of the cake rounded where it has risen. Split the cake in two and fill with buttercream, then spread a layer of buttercream over the surface of the cake to help the sugarpaste stick.

2 Thinly roll out 500g (1lb) of white sugarpaste and cover the cake completely, stretching out any pleats around the sides, smoothing down and trimming excess. Don't worry about an uneven surface, this layer seals in crumbs and will be covered with decoration.

3 Position the cake on the centre of the cake board. Colour 250g (8oz) of sugarpaste red. Thinly roll out the red sugarpaste and place over the top of the cake, encouraging the sugarpaste to lie in folds and pleats for a fabric effect.

4 Using the templates (see page 108) cut out the crown pieces, cutting double the number required (the pieces are stuck back to back to prevent the crown being white on the inside). Stick the backs of the crown pieces together using dabs of royal icing, then stick to the cake sides with royal icing, holding in place for a few seconds until secure.

5 Roll out the remaining white sugarpaste into a strip and stick around the base of the cake with royal icing, pinching the surface to give a fur effect. Stick all the sweets in place around the white sugarpaste with royal icing.

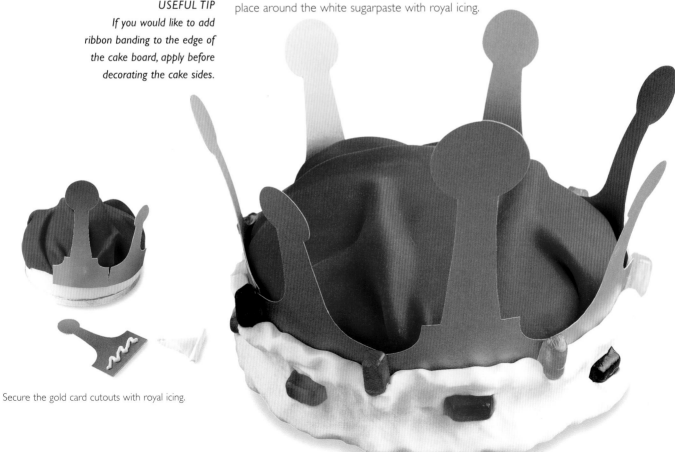

Secure the gold card cutouts with royal icing.

snake pit

One snake for every birthday year will make this cake simply wriggle with fun

MATERIALS
- 23cm (9in) ring-shaped cake, see page 8
- 25cm (10in) round cake board
- 315g (10oz/1¼ cups) buttercream
- 1.5kg (3lb) sugarpaste/rolled fondant
- brown, red, yellow, green, mauve, blue & black food colouring pastes
- icing/confectioners' sugar in a sugar shaker
- sugar glue

EQUIPMENT
- sharp knife
- large rolling pin

1 Trim the crust from the cake with a sharp knife and slice the top flat. Turn the cake over and position the cake on the centre of the cake board. Spread a layer of buttercream over the surface of the cake to help the sugarpaste stick.

2 Colour 750g (1½lb) of sugarpaste brown. Roll out and cover the cake completely, smoothing around the shape and inside the ring. Trim the excess sugarpaste from around the edge of the cake board. Using your hands, indent the sugarpaste all the way around the cake, creating an uneven surface. Model different sized flattened balls with the brown sugarpaste trimmings and stick randomly over the cake.

3 Take five 140g (4½oz) pieces of sugarpaste and colour red, yellow, green, mauve and blue. To make a snake, roll a sausage of coloured sugarpaste with a thin sausage of another colour, tapering in at one end for the tail and rounding off the other end for the head. Holding the head, curl the snake's body around and stick in position with sugar glue.

4 Make all the other snakes in this way. The amounts of sugarpaste quoted will be enough to make eight snakes. Mark each snake's mouth using a knife. To finish, model flattened white sugarpaste ovals for the eyes. Colour a small amount of sugarpaste black and model the pupils, sticking them in place quite close together on the eyes.

Combine two colours to make each snake.

mini monsters

Each party guest can take their own mini monster home with them

MATERIALS

- 25cm (10in) square cake,
  see page 8
- 30cm (12in) round cake board
- 2.25kg (4½lb) sugarpaste/
  rolled fondant
- mauve, red, yellow, orange,
  green, blue, purple & black
  food colouring pastes
- icing/confectioners' sugar
  in a sugar shaker
- 410g (14oz/1¾ cups) buttercream
- sugar glue

EQUIPMENT

- sharp knife
- large rolling pin
- scissors
- 4cm (1½in) circle cutter
- cocktail stick/toothpick

USEFUL TIP

Polish the surface of the sugarpaste with your hands to remove excess icing sugar and to give each cake a sheen.

1 Colour 375g (12oz) of sugarpaste mauve. Using icing sugar to prevent sticking, roll out the mauve sugarpaste and cover the cake board, then put aside to dry.

2 Trim the crust from the cake and slice the top flat. Cut the cake into slightly uneven squares by cutting the cake into three strips, then cutting each strip into four, to get twelve pieces of cake. Trim the corners to round each piece off, then cover each cake with a layer of buttercream to help the sugarpaste stick.

3 To make a mini monster, first split 1.75kg (3½lb) of sugarpaste into six equally sized pieces. Colour the six pieces red, yellow, orange, green, blue and purple. Roll out the red sugarpaste and position a piece of cake on it. Then wrap the sugarpaste around the piece of cake, smoothing the join completely closed.

4 Using scissors, snip up the sugarpaste a couple of times to create tufts of hair. Press the circle cutter in at an angle to indent the smile, then dimple the two corners of each mini monster's mouth with a cocktail stick.

5 Cover the remaining pieces of cake in the same way. Make one more red mini monster, then two each in yellow, orange, green, blue and purple. With the remaining white sugarpaste, model flattened oval shapes for eyes. Colour 15g (½oz) black and roll tiny ball-shaped pupils. Attach the eyes and pupils with sugar glue.

6 To make the feet and hands, model teardrop shapes and flatten slightly. Make two cuts in the wider end and smooth to remove ridges. For the feet, pinch around the centre to indent and flatten under the toes. For hands, pinch to create a wrist. Model uneven ball-shaped noses. Secure all the eyes, noses, feet and hands in place with sugar glue.

7 Carefully position each cake on the cake board. So that each monster can be separated easily when serving, do not use sugar glue when assembling all the monsters on the board, unless the cake has to travel. Don't forget to save a piece for the birthday monster!

Sugarpaste shapes for each monster's hands and feet.

Trim the corners off each square of cake.

Indent a smile with the circle cutter.

dream castle

*A magical dream castle made from
swiss rolls and turrets of marshmallows*

MATERIALS

- 3 x 15cm (6in) swiss rolls/jelly rolls
- 5 mini swiss rolls/jelly rolls
- 25cm (10in) petal-shaped cake board
- 2kg (4lb) sugarpaste/ rolled fondant
- yellow food colouring paste
- icing/confectioners' sugar in a sugar shaker
- 375g (12oz/1½ cups) buttercream
- sugar glue
- 100g (3½oz/½ cup) royal icing
- mini marshmallows
- assorted marshmallow shapes
- silver dragees
- edible pink dusting powder/ petal dust/blossom tint
- edible sparkle powder/ petal dust/blossom tint

EQUIPMENT

- large rolling pin
- sharp knife
- piping bag/tip
- cake smoother (optional)
- medium paintbrush

1 Colour 315g (10oz) of sugarpaste yellow. Using icing sugar to prevent sticking, roll out the yellow sugarpaste and use to cover the cake board, trimming any excess sugarpaste from around the edge. Put the covered board to one side to dry.

2 To create the different sized mini towers, cut one third from a mini swiss roll and sandwich on to the end of another mini swiss roll with buttercream. Spread all the swiss rolls with buttercream to help the sugarpaste stick.

3 Thickly roll out 470g (15oz) of white sugarpaste. Don't be tempted to thinly cover the large swiss rolls to save sugarpaste, as the cakes need the support of a thick layer of sugarpaste. Position one large swiss roll down on to the piece of rolled-out sugarpaste. Cut to size by cutting a straight line in the sugarpaste at either end of the swiss roll.

4 Roll the sugarpaste around the cake, trimming at the join. Moisten the join with sugar glue and smooth closed. To achieve a totally smooth surface, roll the cake over the work surface using a cake smoother. Cover the remaining large swiss rolls in the same way.

5 Make sure that the three large, covered swiss rolls are exactly the same size and are level when upright. Put the royal icing into the piping bag and use it to stick the three large cakes in position on the cake board. Roll out the trimmings of white sugarpaste and cut a piece to fit the top of the three cakes. Place the piece of white sugarpaste on the top of the cakes and trim around the edge, then smooth the joins closed.

6 Press around the top edge of each tower with a sharp knife to indent. Stick mini marshmallows around the top edge of the towers to create the turrets.

7 Cover one end of each mini swiss roll with a piece of white sugarpaste, then roll out the remaining white sugarpaste and cover the sides of the swiss rolls, using the same method as before. Build up pyramids of mini marshmallows to shape roofs for the small towers, securing the marshmallows in place with sugar glue.

continued overleaf!

Sandwich swiss rolls together with buttercream.

Roll a layer of sugarpaste around each large swiss roll.

Place a piece of sugarpaste on top of the tower.

Secure the marshmallows with sugar glue.

8 Make smaller towers with piles of marshmallows to sit on top of the larger towers and at the base of the main cake. Secure all the towers in place on the cake board with royal icing. Place assorted marshmallow shapes around the towers to decorate.

9 Create the windows and door handles using silver dragees, pressing each one gently into the sugarpaste and marshmallow pieces. Stick a dragee on the top of each roof, then sprinkle some over the cake board. When the cake is dry, use a paintbrush to dust the cake with the edible pink dusting powder and sparkle powder.

Dust the whole cake with sparkle powder.

When the castle is finished, decorate the board with different-sized marshmallows.

smiling sun

This smiley sun has got his hat on, and he is ready to come out to play

MATERIALS
- 2 x 1 litre (2 pint/5 cup) bowl-shaped cakes, see page 8
- 35cm (14in) round cake board
- 2kg (4lb) sugarpaste/rolled fondant
- blue, yellow & black food colouring pastes
- icing/confectioners' sugar in a sugar shaker
- 280g (9oz/1 generous cup) buttercream
- sugar glue

EQUIPMENT
- large rolling pin
- sharp knife
- cake smoother
- template, see page 108

Using the template, cut out the sunglasses.

1 Colour 500g (1lb) of sugarpaste pale blue. Using icing sugar to prevent sticking, roll out and cover the cake board completely, trimming excess from around edge. Trim the crust from each cake and slice the tops flat. Sandwich the two cakes together to make a ball, then spread buttercream over the surface to help the sugarpaste stick.

2 Colour 1kg (2lb) of sugarpaste yellow. Roll out and use to cover the cake completely, smoothing down around the shape and underneath. Cut away any excess pleats of sugarpaste and smooth the joins closed. Position the cake on the centre of the cake board and smooth the surface with a cake smoother.

3 To indent a wide grin, gently press in the rim of the ovenproof bowl that the cake was baked in, then smooth with your finger at each end for the corners of the mouth. Colour 45g (1½oz) of sugarpaste black. Roll out the black sugarpaste and cut out the sunglasses, using the template (see page 108). Stick in place with a little sugar glue.

4 For the handkerchief hat, thinly roll out 155g (5oz) of white sugarpaste and cut an oblong measuring 12 x 8cm (5 x 3in). Position on top of the sun, pleating the sides by pinching carefully. Make little curly teardrop shapes for the handkerchief corners, then roll small balls for each tie. To make the clouds, roll different sized balls of white sugarpaste, five for the front cloud and four for the back, then roll out the remaining white sugarpaste and cover the clouds completely, smoothing around the shape.

drummer boy

This cake is sure to create a big bang when presented at the party table

MATERIALS

- 2 x 15cm (6in) round cakes, see page 8
- 25cm (10in) round cake board
- 1.5kg (3lb) sugarpaste/ rolled fondant
- blue, black, red & cream food colouring pastes
- icing/confectioners' sugar in a sugar shaker
- 375g (12oz/1½ cups) buttercream
- sugar glue
- silver dragees

EQUIPMENT

- large rolling pin
- sharp knife
- cake smoother
- silver embroidery thread
- cocktail stick/ toothpick
- small circle cutter
- 2 lollipop sticks

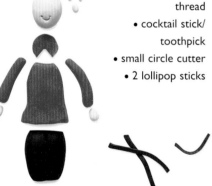

Sugarpaste shapes for the soldier.

1 Colour 315g (10oz) of sugarpaste blue. Roll out and cover the cake board, then put aside to dry. Trim the crust from each cake and slice the tops flat. Sandwich the two cakes together with buttercream, then spread a layer over the surface of the cake.

2 Roll out 600g (1¼lb) of white sugarpaste and cut a strip to fit around the cake sides. Dust with icing sugar, then carefully roll up. Position the end against the cake sides, then unroll around the cake. Secure the join with sugar glue and rub gently to close. Roll out 250g (8oz) of white. Position the top of the cake down on to it and cut around. Turn the cake the other way up and position on the board. Rub gently with a cake smoother.

3 Colour 250g (8oz) of sugarpaste black. Roll out 100g (3½oz) and cut a strip to fit round the base of the cake. Roll up, then stick around the cake using sugar glue. Make a band for the top edge in the same way. To stick the silver thread in place, moisten the side of the black band where the thread is to be inserted. Push the thread into the sugarpaste with a cocktail stick. Press the thread into the band at the top and bottom, creating a zigzag pattern. Stick silver dragees at each point. Colour 75g (2½oz) red. Split 15g (½oz) in half and roll balls for the drum sticks. Using sugar glue, push the lollipop sticks into each and put aside to dry.

4 To make the soldier's shoes, split 7g (¼oz) of black sugarpaste in half and model two teardrop shapes, sticking the points together. For the trousers, model a teardrop shape using 30g (1oz), flatten slightly and cut the top and bottom straight. Mark a line down the front to separate the legs, then stick on to the shoes. To make the jacket, model a teardrop shape with 45g (1½oz) of red, flatten slightly and cut the top and bottom straight. Pinch around the base to hollow out so it sits neatly over the trousers and pinch at the waist to narrow. Stick in place on the trousers and against the cake. Make two sausage-shaped arms, then flatten a small ball, cutting a 'v' from one side to make a collar.

5 Colour some white trimmings cream to make the head, nose and hands, marking a smile with the circle cutter. Shape a black hat, hollowing out at the base to sit on his head. Cut thin strips using black, then stick everything in place with sugar glue. Decorate with two silver dragees. Position the drum sticks on the cake. Remove the thread before serving.

Unroll the strip of sugarpaste around the cake.

Place the cake on the sugarpaste and cut around.

Push the silver thread in with a cocktail stick.

party bags

Children will be thrilled to take these bags home at the end of the party

MATERIALS
- 20cm (8in) square cake, see page 8
- 30cm (12in) round cake board
- 2kg (4lb) sugarpaste/ rolled fondant
- green, blue, red, golden brown & black food colouring pastes
- icing/confectioners' sugar in a sugar shaker
- 375g (12oz/1½ cups) buttercream
- sugar glue
- black food colouring pen
- lollipops
- sugar-coated chocolates

EQUIPMENT
- rolling pin
- sharp knife
- large petal cutter
- miniature circle cutter
- cocktail stick/toothpick

1 Colour 375g (12oz) of sugarpaste green. Using icing sugar to prevent sticking, roll out and cover the cake board, trimming the excess sugarpaste from around the edge. Put the covered board aside to dry. Trim the crust from the cake and slice the top flat. Cut the cake into nine equal sized squares, as in the photograph below. Spread each of the squares of cake with buttercream to help the sugarpaste stick.

2 Cover the top of one piece of cake by rolling out 15g (½oz) of white sugarpaste and placing the top of the square down on to it, then cutting around. Cover the top of all the other squares in the same way. To make a bag, roll out 155g (5oz) of white sugarpaste and cut a straight edge. Place the bottom edge of the square on this line. Cut the top of the sugarpaste in a straight line 2.5cm (1in) above the cake. Wrap the white sugarpaste around the cake, trimming any excess at the join. Stick the join together with sugar glue, then gently rub the join closed. Cover all the other squares in the same way.

3 Colour some sugarpaste trimmings red and blue. To decorate the bags, thinly roll out the pieces of green, red and blue sugarpaste and cut out balloon shapes with the petal cutter, sticking in them place on the sides of the bags with sugar glue.

4 Colour 410g (13oz) of sugarpaste golden brown. To make one teddy, roll 22g (¾oz) into a ball for a body. Roll 15g (½oz) into another ball for a head and stick on to the body with sugar glue. With 7g (¼oz), shape two oval-shaped feet, make a ball-shaped muzzle, two tiny ears and two sausage-shaped arms. Press a cocktail stick into each ear to indent. Mark a line on the muzzle using a knife. Press the miniature circle cutter in at an angle to indent the smile and dimple by pressing the tip of a cocktail stick into each corner.

5 Make eight more teddy bears in this way, turning their heads slightly to look in different directions. Colour some of the sugarpaste trimmings black and shape all the little triangular noses. Fill each bag with a teddy, a lollipop and a few sugar-coated chocolates. When the cakes are dry, draw in fine lines for the balloon strings on each bag with the black food colouring pen. Draw dots for eyes. Finally, position the cakes on the cake board, ensuring that the sides with the balloons are facing outwards.

Sugarpaste shapes for the teddy bears.

Cover the squares of cake with buttercream.

Wrap white sugarpaste around each piece of cake.

alien spaceship

*Space buffs will certainly give this
alien creation permission to land*

MATERIALS

- 2 litre (4 pint/10 cup) bowl-shaped cake,
see page 9
- 35cm (14in) round cake board
- 1kg (2lb) sugarpaste/
rolled fondant
- mauve, black & green
food colouring pastes
- icing/confectioners' sugar
in a sugar shaker
- 185g (6oz/¾ cup) buttercream
- 60g (2oz/¼ cup) royal icing
- strands of liquorice/licorice
- fruit-flavoured jelly sweets/candies

EQUIPMENT

- large rolling pin
- sharp knife
- cake smoother
- cocktail sticks/toothpicks
- small circle cutter
- piping bag

*USEFUL TIP
A sprinkling of icing sugar
when rolling out sugarpaste
helps prevent it sticking
to the work surface.*

1 Colour 750g (1½lb) of sugarpaste mauve. Roll out 470g (15oz) and cover the cake board, then put aside to dry. Trim the crust from the cake and slice the top flat. Turn the cake upside down. Spread with a layer of buttercream to help the sugarpaste stick before positioning the cake on the centre of the cake board.

2 Roll out the remaining mauve sugarpaste and cover the top of the cake only. Trim away the excess sugarpaste, leaving a strip of uncovered cake around the base approximately 5cm (2in) wide. Smooth the surface with a cake smoother.

3 Colour 140g (4½oz) of sugarpaste black, roll it out thinly and cut a strip to fit the gap around the base of the cake. With the mauve sugarpaste trimmings, cut narrow strips to mark the windows and stick them in place with a little royal icing.

4 Colour the remaining sugarpaste green. To make each alien, roll a ball of sugarpaste, pulling down a neck and carefully pinching all the way round until long and thin. Put the alien on to the work surface, then push in the tip of a cocktail stick to mark two nostrils. Press in twice at the top to make two holes for the long antennae to slot into. Don't make the antennae until all the aliens are in position on the cake.

5 To mark the mouth, press in the circle cutter at an angle. Roll tiny balls of black sugarpaste for the eyes. Make all the other aliens, some larger than others, and secure them in position with royal icing.

6 Make the aliens' antennae by rolling a long, thin sausage of green sugarpaste and cutting it into short lengths. Slot the antennae into the holes. Stick a black ball on to the end of each of the antennae, securing everything in place with tiny dots of royal icing.

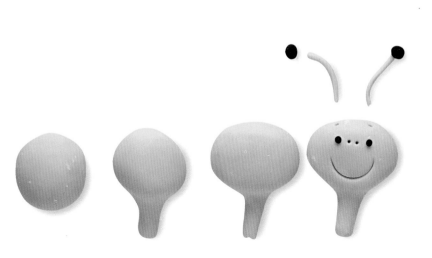

Mould a ball of green sugarpaste to create each alien's head, neck and ears.

7 Stick strips of liquorice and fruit-flavoured jelly sweets around the outside edge of the cake board using royal icing. Cut two small lengths of liquorice and push them into the top of the spaceship to create the aerial. Cut a small hole in two of the sweets and slot them carefully on to the ends of each of the liquorice strands. This spaceship and its alien occupants are now ready for take off!

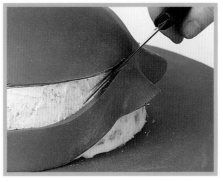

Trim a strip of sugarpaste from the base of the cake.

Decorate the edge of the cake board with sweets.

Ensure that the surface of the cake is kept smooth by using a cake smoother at all stages.

dog & bone

An unusual and very simple cake for any dog lover. No baking required!

MATERIALS
- 1 swiss roll/jelly roll
- 4 fairy cakes/cup cakes
- 30 x 25cm (12 x 10in) oblong cake board
- 1.5kg (3lb) sugarpaste/ rolled fondant
- black & red food colouring pastes
- icing/confectioners' sugar in a sugar shaker
- sugar glue
- 250g (8oz/1 cup) buttercream

EQUIPMENT
- large rolling pin
- sharp knife
- cocktail stick/toothpick

USEFUL TIP
Make sure that the covered cake board is completely dry before covering the cake with sugarpaste.

1 Colour 470g (15oz) of sugarpaste black. Roll out 440g (14oz) and cover the cake board, trimming any excess from around the edge. Thinly roll out 60g (2oz) of white sugarpaste and cut thin strips for the cake board, securing in place with sugar glue. Colour 75g (2½oz) of sugarpaste red. Thinly roll out and cut slightly wider strips than before to complete the checked pattern, then put aside to dry.

2 Position the swiss roll diagonally on the cake board, with two fairy cakes at either end, to form the dog's bone. Spread a thin layer of buttercream over the surface of the cakes to help the sugarpaste stick and to fill in the gaps between the cakes.

3 Roll out 625g (1¼lb) of white sugarpaste, using icing sugar to prevent the sugarpaste sticking to the work surface, and cover the cakes completely, smoothing around the shape of the bone. Trim carefully around the base, tucking the sugarpaste underneath.

4 To make the dog, first model a thick sausage using 140g (4½oz) of white sugarpaste. Following the stages in the photograph below, first make a cut at one end to separate the front legs, then smooth away the ridges and round off each front paw. Pinch the body all the way round to create a dip in the middle. Model one black and one white back leg, using 30g (1oz) of sugarpaste for each. Press the top of each leg flat, then stick in position using sugar glue. Press in with the side of a cocktail stick to mark the lines on each paw.

5 Using 15g (½oz) of red sugarpaste, model a flattened ball and stick on to the dog for his collar. Then roll a 90g (3oz) ball of white for the dog's head and pinch slightly to narrow the top. Model two flattened teardrop shapes for the dog's muzzle and two tiny flattened ovals for eyes. Mark holes in the muzzle using the tip of a cocktail stick.

6 Press on a black eye patch, spreading it out until completely flat, then stick on the two white eyes and black pupils. Shape a wide, triangular nose and two teardrop-shaped ears, then model a tongue with red sugarpaste. Stick these pieces on to the dog's head, then secure the head on the red collar with sugar glue. To finish, roll a sausage tapering to a point for a tail, and stick different sized black patches on the dog's body.

The dog's head, ears and collar.

Model the sugarpaste to create the dog's body and legs.

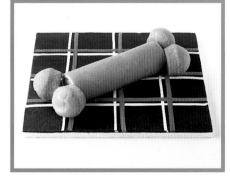

Place the cakes on the board to form the bone.

make-up bag

If short of time, why not scatter the cake board with real girl's make-up?

MATERIALS
- 18cm (7in) round cake, see page 8
- 25cm (10in) round cake board
- 1.25kg (2½lb) sugarpaste/ rolled fondant
- pink & mauve food colouring pastes
- icing/confectioners' sugar in a sugar shaker
- 315g (10oz/1¼ cups) buttercream
- dark blue, dark purple, gold, dark pink, silver, pink, mauve & white edible sparkle powders/ petal dusts/blossom tints
- sugar glue

EQUIPMENT
- large rolling pin
- sharp knife
- small & large flower cutters
- 4.5cm (1¾in) circle cutter
- template, see page 109

Fill the tubs with different coloured sparkle powders.

1 Colour 315g (10oz) of sugarpaste pale pink. Roll out and cover the cake board. Trim excess from around the edge, then put aside to dry. Trim the crust from the cake and slice the top flat. Cut a 3.5cm (1½in) wedge from one edge of the cake to form the base of the make-up bag. Spread a layer of buttercream over the surface. Roll out 220g (7oz) of white sugarpaste. Place the back of the cake down on the sugarpaste and cut around. Cover the front in the same way. Colour 100g (3½oz) of sugarpaste mauve. Thinly roll out 30g (1oz) and cut a strip to cover the opening around the top of the cake.

2 Roll out 200g (6½oz) of white sugarpaste and cut two strips to cover the top of the cake, leaving the mauve inner strip showing. For the zip, press the tip of a knife along each side, then mark a line for the zip edge. Roll the white trimmings into two long thin sausages and use to hide the joins, then position the cake on the cake board. Thinly roll out 30g (1oz) of white sugarpaste and cut ten flowers with the large flower cutter, sticking in place with sugar glue. Using pink sugarpaste trimmings, model little flattened balls and use to fill each flower centre. Make another flower for the zip trim, using the small flower cutter.

3 To make the make-up, colour 45g (1½oz) of sugarpaste dark pink and 22g (¾oz) pale purple. For the mirror, thinly roll out dark pink and cut out a heart, using the template (see page 109), and a circle. Stick together with sugar glue, then stick on the board. With the remaining dark pink, roll a sausage for the base of the make-up tube and a tiny sausage for the applicator handle. Shape the eye shadow tub by pressing down into a ball of sugarpaste and smoothing around to create a dip. With the pale purple, shape another tub, the top of the lipstick, a small sausage for the applicator and the brush bristles, marking with a knife.

4 With mauve, make another eye shadow tub, the lipstick tube pieces and lid, the brush handle, a ball-shaped nail varnish bottle and a pencil tip. With white, make two more eye shadow tubs, the lid for the nail varnish tapering to a point, the sausage-shaped make-up tube lid and pencil, and all the applicator tips. Stick together with sugar glue. Rub patches of pink and mauve sparkle powder over the the cake, then brush with white sparkle powder. Fill the eye shadow tubs with sparkle powders and dip the applicator at either end. To finish, brush blue sparkle over the nail varnish bottle and silver over the mirror, lids and pencil.

Place a strip of mauve along the top of the cake.

Indent the zip with the tip of a sharp knife.

Brush silver sparkle powder on to the mirror.

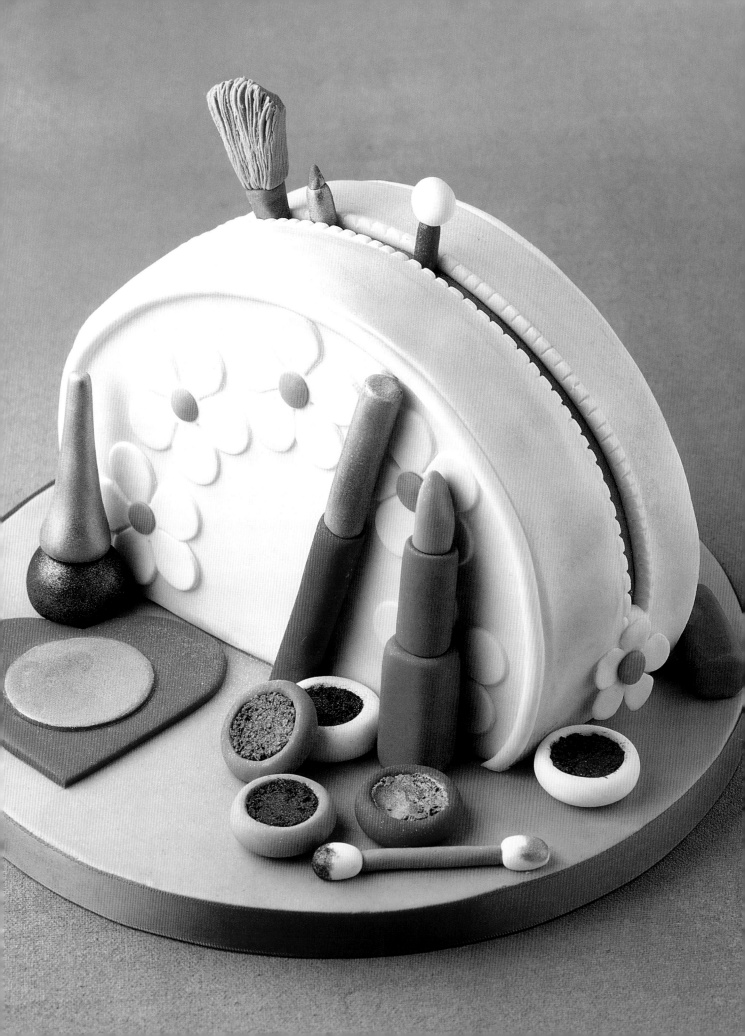

giant cup cake

A giant cake with the cutest teddy bear on top – a must for any small child

MATERIALS

- 22 x 9.5cm (8¾ x 3¾in) brioche-shaped cake, see page 8
- 25cm (10in) round cake board
- 1.5kg (3lb) sugarpaste/rolled fondant
- mauve, golden brown, red & green food colouring pastes
- icing/confectioners' sugar in a sugar shaker
- 220g (7oz/1 cup) buttercream
- sugar glue

EQUIPMENT

- large rolling pin
- sharp knife
- scissors
- bone tool
- small circle cutter
- cocktail stick/toothpick
- medium & large blossom cutters, see page 5

USEFUL TIP

Make sure that the buttercream is still soft on the sides of the cake before covering the cake with white sugarpaste, or the sugarpaste may start to come away from the cake sides when turned back over.

1 Colour 315g (10oz) of sugarpaste mauve. Roll out and cover the cake board, trimming excess from around the edge. Put the covered board aside to dry.

2 Turn the cake upside down and spread the bottom and sides with a layer of buttercream to help the sugarpaste stick. Roll out 750g (1½lb) of white sugarpaste and cover the cake completely, smoothing around the shape and into the grooves in the side of the cake. With scissors, cut a neat edge about 1cm (½in) longer than the cake edge. Carefully turn the cake back over and position on the centre of the cake board.

3 Roll out 185g (6oz) of white sugarpaste and use to cover the top of the cake, sticking in position with buttercream. Smooth the edge to round off and create a wavy effect.

4 To make the teddy bear, first colour 185g (6oz) of sugarpaste golden brown. Roll 60g (2oz) into a ball-shaped body. With 75g (2½oz), make a head and stick it in place using sugar glue. With the remaining piece, make two teardrop-shaped arms, flattened ovals for feet, an oval muzzle pressed flat and two ball-shaped ears.

5 Indent each ear using the small end of the bone tool. Indent the smile using the circle cutter pressed in at an angle and dimple the corners with a cocktail stick, then mark a line with the knife. Roll two white, oval-shaped eyes. Colour a tiny amount of sugarpaste black and make a nose and two pupils.

6 Model a cone from the white sugarpaste trimmings and stick it on top of the teddy's head. Colour the remaining sugarpaste red and green. Roll a small ball of red to make the cherry, pressing in the top with a cocktail stick to indent.

7 Thinly roll out the rest of the red sugarpaste and cut flowers using the blossom cutters. Stick the flowers around the edge of the cake board and over the white sugarpaste around the cake. With green sugarpaste, model the tiny teardrop-shaped leaves. Finally, roll out and cut red and green strips from the trimmings to decorate the hat.

Sugarpaste shapes for the teddy bear.

Trim the edges of the sugarpaste.

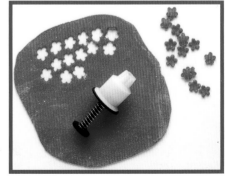

Cut flowers using a blossom cutter.

jewellery box

This pretty jewellery box will bring a gasp of delight from any little girl

MATERIALS
- 20cm (8in) square cake, see page 8
- 30cm (12in) petal-shaped cake board
- 1.4kg (2lb 13oz) sugarpaste/ rolled fondant
- blue & pink food colouring pastes
- icing/confectioners' sugar in a sugar shaker
- 410g (13oz/1⅔ cups) buttercream
- sugar glue
- mints, sweet/candy necklaces, mini sweets/candies & silver dragees
- edible pink sparkle powder/ petal dust/blossom tint

EQUIPMENT
- large rolling pin
- sharp knife
- cake smoother
- template, see page 110
- medium paintbrush

1 Colour 375g (12oz) of sugarpaste blue. Using icing sugar to prevent sticking, roll out the blue sugarpaste and cover the cake board. Trim any excess from around the edge, then put aside to dry. Trim the crust from the cake and slice the top flat.

2 Cut the cake in half, then sandwich one half on top of the other using buttercream. Spread a layer of buttercream over the surface of the cake to help the sugarpaste stick.

3 Roll out the remaining white sugarpaste. Position one side of the cake down on to the sugarpaste and cut around the shape with a sharp knife. Cover all sides of the cake in the same way, smoothing the joins closed. Cover the top in the same way, but cut the sugarpaste slightly wider than the actual cake to create a lip at the front.

4 Position the cake on the centre of the cake board and smooth the surface with a cake smoother. Using your finger, smooth slight dips around the lid to create a wavy effect.

5 Colour the sugarpaste trimmings pink. Roll out and cut two ballet shoes using the template (see page 110). Smooth around the edge of each shoe to round off, then press in the centre to create a dip and to outline the inside of each shoe. Thinly roll out the remaining pink sugarpaste and cut strips for the shoe ribbons. Stick the shoes and ribbons in position on the front of the cake with sugar glue.

6 Arrange all the different types of candy jewellery around the cake, securing them in position with sugar glue. Build up the mint necklace from the cake board up, so each mint is supported by the previous one. Stick with sugar glue, pressing firmly in place. Create a ring with a loop of white sugarpaste, and use a few silver dragees to create a sparkling jewel. When the cake is dry, use the paintbrush to dust with edible pink sparkle powder.

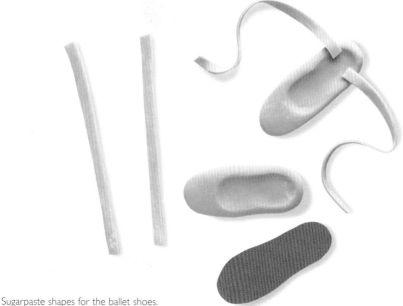

Sugarpaste shapes for the ballet shoes.

Cut the sugarpaste to fit the sides of the cake.

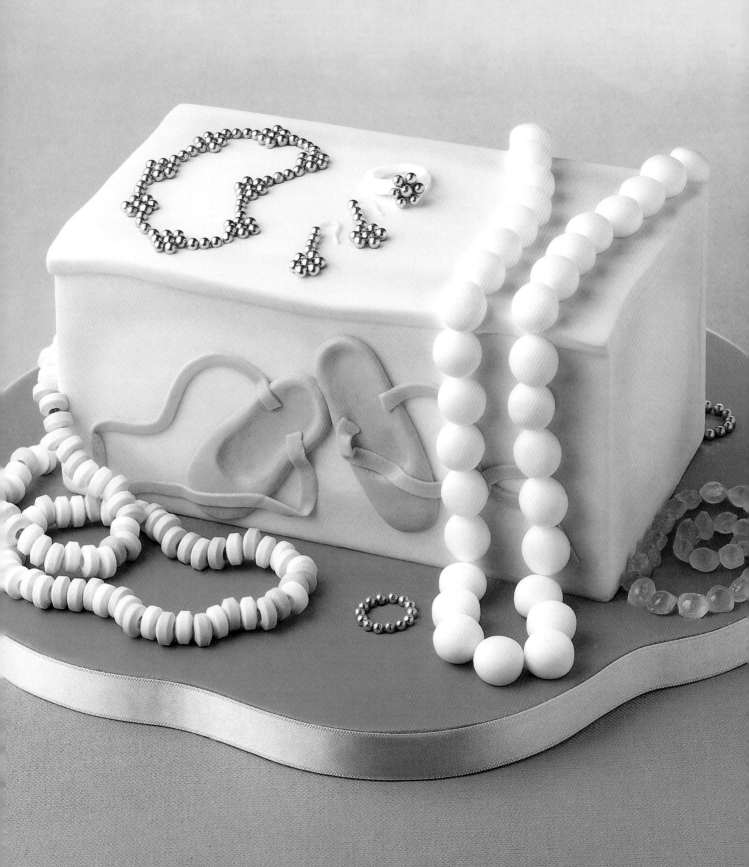

lovable ladybird

With its cheeky grin, this ladybird is sure to be a favourite birthday treat

MATERIALS

- 2 litre (4 pint/10 cup) bowl-shaped cake, see page 8
- 30cm (12in) round cake board
- 1.35kg (2¾lb) sugarpaste/ rolled fondant
- green, red, black & yellow food colouring pastes
- icing/confectioners' sugar in a sugar shaker
- 185g (6oz/¾ cup) buttercream
- sugar glue
- lengths of liquorice/licorice

EQUIPMENT

- sharp knife
- large rolling pin
- 4cm (1½in) circle cutter

USEFUL TIP

When sticking the ladybird's head to the body, do not use too much sugar glue as it could slide out of place.

1 Colour 375g (12oz) of sugarpaste green. Using icing sugar to prevent sticking, roll out the green sugarpaste and cover the cake board. Put the covered board aside to dry.

2 Trim the crust from the bowl-shaped cake and slice the top of the cake flat, using a sharp knife. Turn the cake upside down and then spread a layer of buttercream over the surface of the cake to help the sugarpaste stick.

3 Colour 625g (1¼lb) of sugarpaste red. Roll out and cover the cake, smoothing around the shape, then trim any excess from around the edge. Position the cake on the cake board. Using the back of a knife, mark a line down the centre of the ladybird's back.

4 Colour 155g (5oz) of sugarpaste black. Roll 125g (4oz) into a ball-shaped head. Stick in position using a little sugar glue then, with the circle cutter, press in at an angle to indent the smile. Dimple the corners of the smile using your finger.

5 Push two pieces of liquorice into the top of the ladybird's head and stick a small ball of black sugarpaste on the end of each antenna. Roll two tiny amounts of white sugarpaste into balls and press on to the face for the eyes.

6 With the remaining black sugarpaste, model two pupils, then roll out and cut six circles for the spots to decorate the ladybird's back. Secure on the cake with sugar glue.

7 Colour the remaining sugarpaste yellow. Model long, yellow teardrop shapes for petals, pressing each shape flat but still keeping them fairly thick. Stick the petals in position around the ladybird, making sure they do not hang over the cake board edge.

8 Make smaller and shorter yellow petals for a second layer, encouraging the petals to bend, as in the photograph opposite, then secure in place with sugar glue.

Sugarpaste shapes for the ladybird's head.

Model petals from pieces of yellow sugarpaste.

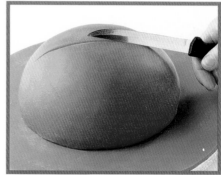
Mark a line down the centre of the cake.

spooky tower

The perfect cake for any would-be ghostbuster who likes being spooked

MATERIALS

- 20cm (8in) square cake, see page 8
- 20cm (8in) round cake board
- 1.5kg (3lb) sugarpaste/rolled fondant
- dark blue, black & pink food colouring pastes
- icing/confectioners' sugar in a sugar shaker
- 375g (12oz/1½ cups) buttercream
- sugar glue
- edible sparkle powder/petal dust/blossom tint

EQUIPMENT

- large rolling pin
- sharp knife
- cake smoother
- small square cutter
- fine paintbrush

1 Colour 375g (12oz) of sugarpaste dark blue. Roll out 280g (9oz) and cover the cake board, then put aside to dry. Trim the crust from the cake and slice the top flat. Cut the cake into four equal sized squares. Trim each square to create four circles. Sandwich together with buttercream, then spread the surface of the cake with a layer of buttercream.

2 Colour 1kg (2lb) of sugarpaste pale blue-grey using a tiny amount of the blue and black food colourings. Position the cake down on to 875g (1¾lb) of rolled-out blue-grey sugarpaste. Roll it around the cake, trimming any excess from the join and at either end. Stick the join together with sugar glue, then rub gently with the cake smoother to close. Roll the cake carefully on the work surface to smooth out any wrinkles.

3 Position the cake on the board, sticking in place with sugar glue. Use a cake smoother to polish the surface. Roll out the remaining dark blue sugarpaste and cut a circle to fit the top of the tower. Remove pieces of sugarpaste to create the door and windows. Thinly roll out dark blue sugarpaste and cut inserts for the door and windows.

4 Roll out the remaining blue-grey sugarpaste and cut a 5cm (2in) deep strip. Using the square cutter, cut out the turrets. Moisten around the top edge of the cake with a small amount of sugar glue. Carefully roll up the turret and position it against the top of the cake, then unroll it all the way around. Glue the join and smooth closed.

5 Colour the grey sugarpaste trimmings slightly different shades by adding tiny amounts of blue, black and pink food colourings. Shape flattened balls of paste and stick over the tower and around the door and windows. Cut wedges for the window sills. Create the staircase by making the lowest stair the thickest, each further stair getting gradually thinner.

6 Model a long, tapering sausage of white sugarpaste for the ghostly tail and stick in position around the cake, twisting up to the top window. Make all the ghosts with white sugarpaste and stick in place with sugar glue, holding for a few seconds until secure. Model their eyes using flattened balls of white. Using the fine paintbrush, paint the eyes and mouths with the black food colouring. Brush the edible sparkle powder over the cake.

Shape white sugarpaste to create the ghosts.

Cut the cake into four equal sized circles.

Roll the blue-grey sugarpaste around the cake.

Cut the turrets with the small square cutter.

cute chick

A perfect cake for a small child's birthday or as a bright Easter treat

MATERIALS

- 1 x 2 litre (4 pint/10 cup) & 1 x 0.5 litre (1 pint/2½ cup) bowl-shaped cakes, see page 9
- 30cm (12in) round cake board
- 1.8kg (3lb 10oz) sugarpaste/ rolled fondant
- green, yellow, orange & black food colouring pastes
- icing/confectioners' sugar in a sugar shaker
- 440g (14oz/1¾ cups) buttercream
- sugar glue

EQUIPMENT

- large rolling pin
- sharp knife
- cake smoother

USEFUL TIP

When a large piece of sugarpaste is rolled out, lift by folding it over the rolling pin. This will make it easier to position the sugarpaste on the cake.

1 Colour 375g (12oz) of sugarpaste green. Using icing sugar to prevent sticking, roll out the green sugarpaste and cover the cake board, trimming the excess from around the edge. Set aside to dry. Trim the crust from the cake, keeping the rounded top on each where the cakes have risen. Cut two layers in the large cake and one layer in the smaller cake. Sandwich both cakes back together with buttercream.

2 Turn each cake upside down (the cakes are decorated this way up) and spread with a layer of buttercream to help the sugarpaste stick. Colour 1.25kg (2½lb) of sugarpaste yellow. Using 30g (1oz), pad the top of the smaller cake to heighten the top of the head.

3 Roll out 625g (1¼lb) of yellow sugarpaste and cover the larger cake completely, smoothing around the shape and tucking the sugarpaste underneath. Roll out 375g (12oz) of yellow sugarpaste and cover the smaller cake in the same way. Position the cakes on the board with the smaller cake on top, using sugar glue to secure them in place. Smooth the surface of both cakes with a cake smoother.

4 For the wings, roll six long teardrop shapes of yellow sugarpaste. Stick three on to each side of the chick's body, graduating down in size and curving up around the back. Model three smaller yellow teardrop shapes for the tail and three teardrop shapes for the hair tuft. Stick these pieces in place, curling up the points.

5 Colour a tiny amount of sugarpaste black, then colour the remaining piece of sugarpaste orange. Split the orange sugarpaste into three equal sized pieces. From two pieces, shape two ovals, pinching four times along the top of each to make webbed feet, as in the photograph below. Stick in position, pressing the centre of each to indent.

6 Roll a sausage with the remaining orange sugarpaste, then roll on either side of the centre to create dips to shape the beak. Stick on the chick's face, just below half-way. Finally, make the two oval-shaped eyes by rolling two small balls of black sugarpaste. Stick in place in the centre of the face, quite close together, securing with a little sugar glue.

Sugarpaste shapes for the chick's webbed feet.

Sandwich the cakes together with buttercream.

Cover both cakes with yellow sugarpaste.

templates

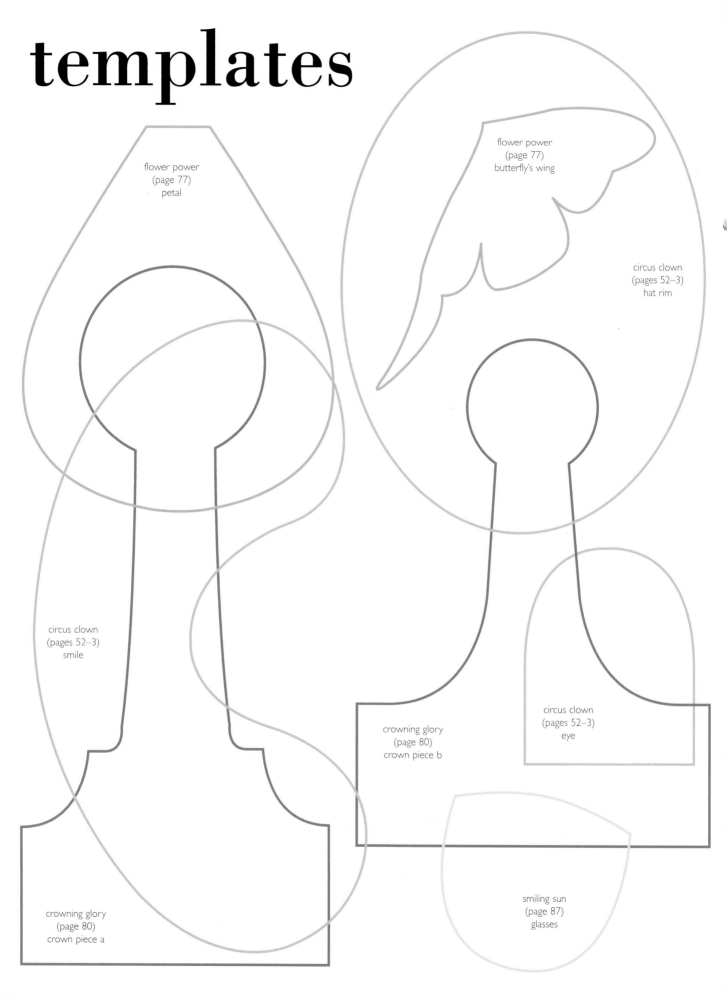

flower power
(page 77)
petal

flower power
(page 77)
butterfly's wing

circus clown
(pages 52–3)
hat rim

circus clown
(pages 52–3)
smile

circus clown
(pages 52–3)
eye

crowning glory
(page 80)
crown piece b

crowning glory
(page 80)
crown piece a

smiling sun
(page 87)
glasses

farm tractor
(pages 16–18)
front grille

farm tractor
(pages 16–18)
side grille

skull & crossbones
(page 59)
eyes

make-up bag
(pages 96–7)
heart mirror

skull & crossbones
(page 59)
nose

fairy toadstool
(pages 26–7)
door

Little Bo Peep
(pages 38–9)
bush a

fairy toadstool
(pages 26–7)
window

skull & crossbones
(page 59)
mouth

Little Bo Peep
(pages 38–9)
bush b

Little Bo Peep
(pages 38–9)
bush c

Little Bo Peep
(pages 38–9)
apron

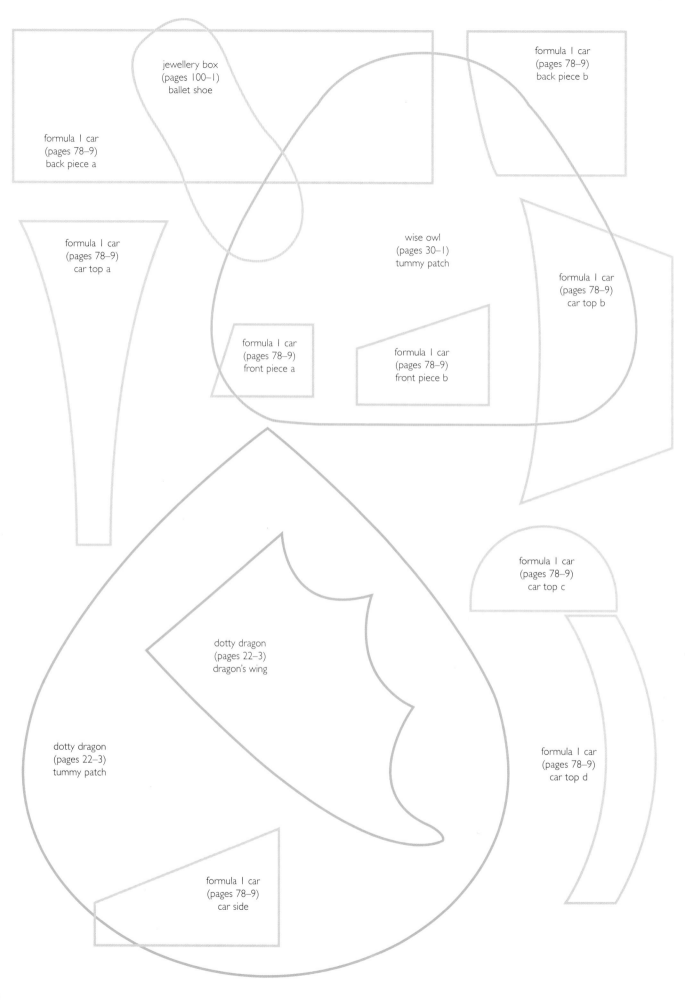

jewellery box
(pages 100–1)
ballet shoe

formula 1 car
(pages 78–9)
back piece b

formula 1 car
(pages 78–9)
back piece a

formula 1 car
(pages 78–9)
car top a

wise owl
(pages 30–1)
tummy patch

formula 1 car
(pages 78–9)
car top b

formula 1 car
(pages 78–9)
front piece a

formula 1 car
(pages 78–9)
front piece b

formula 1 car
(pages 78–9)
car top c

dotty dragon
(pages 22–3)
dragon's wing

dotty dragon
(pages 22–3)
tummy patch

formula 1 car
(pages 78–9)
car top d

formula 1 car
(pages 78–9)
car side

110

dedication

For Lewis, Laura, Shaun, Daniel, Sarah, Rhys, David and Craig

acknowledgements

The author and publishers would like to thank the following suppliers:

Culpitt Cake Art
Culpitt Ltd.
Jubilee Industrial Estate
Ashington
Northumberland, NE63 8UQ
tel: 01670 814 545

Guy, Paul and Co. Ltd.
Unit B4, Foundry Way
Little End Road
Eaton Socon
Cambs
PE19 3JH

Renshaw Scott Ltd.
Crown Street
Liverpool
L8 7RF
The sugarpaste/rolled fondant used in this book was Renshaw's Regalice.

Squires Kitchen
Squires House
3 Waverley Lane
Farnham
Surrey, GU9 8BB
tel: 01252 711 749

Other distributors and retailers:

Confectionery Supplies
31 Lower Cathedral Road
Riverside
Cardiff
South Glamorgan
CF1 8LU
tel: 01222 372 161

Beryl's Cake Decorating & Pastry Supplies
P.O. Box 1584
N. Springfield
VA22151-0584 USA
tel: 1 800 488 2749
fax: 1 703 750 3779

Cakes & Co.
25 Rock Hill
Blackrock Village
Co. Dublin
Ireland
tel: 353 1 283 6544

Cake Decorators' Supplies
Shop 1
770 George Street
Sydney 2001
Australia
tel: 61 2 9212 4050

First published 1999 by Merehurst Ltd., Ferry House, 51–57 Lacy Road, Putney, London, SW15 1PR

Copyright © Debra Brown 1999
Photography copyright © Merehurst Ltd.

Debra Brown has asserted her right under the Copyright, Designs and Patents Act, 1988

ISBN 1 85391 855 5

Commissioning Editor:
Barbara Croxford
Project Editor:
Rowena Curtis
Design Concept & Art Direction:
Laura Jackson
Design:
Axis Design
Photography:
Clive Streeter
Publishing Manager:
Fia Fornari
Production Manager:
Lucy Byrne
CEO & Publisher:
Anne Wilson
International Sales Director:
Kevin Lagden
Marketing & Sales Director:
Kathryn Harvey

Colour separation by Colourscan, Singapore
Printed in Hong Kong by Toppan Printing

index